The Shirtmaking Workbook

Pattern, Design, and Construction Resources

David Page Coffin

Creative Publishing
international

Creative Publishing
international

Copyright © 2015 Creative Publishing international
Text © 2015 David Page Coffin
Photography © 2015 David Page Coffin
Illustration © 2015 David Page Coffin

First published in the United States of America by
Creative Publishing international, a division of
Quarto Publishing Group USA Inc.
400 First Avenue North
Suite 400
Minneapolis, MN 55401
1-800-328-3895
www.creativepub.com
Visit www.Craftside.net for a behind-the-scenes peek at our crafty world!

ISBN: 978-1-58923-826-8

Digital edition published in 2015
eISBN: 978-1-62788-274-3

10 9 8 7 6 5 4 3 2 1

Library of Congress Cataloging-in-Publication Data available

Copy Editor: Karen Levy
Proofreader: Julie Grady
Cover and Book Design: Laura H. Couallier, Laura Herrmann Design
Page Layout: Megan Jones Design
Illustrations: David Page Coffin
Photographs: David Page Coffin
Cover Image: Glenn Scott Photography

Photo Credits
Pages 79-81: The Metropolitan Museum of Art, Gift of Estate of H.R.H. Duke of Windsor and the Duchess of Windsor, 1986 (1986.295.17) / (1986.295.16). Photographs by the author; published with permission of the Metropolitan Museum of Art
Page 79: Photographs by the author; published with permission of the Metropolitan Museum of Art

Printed in China

Dedication

To my brilliant and gentle father, David Page Coffin, who is maybe somewhere now at last understanding why the thing I most fondly recall from all the superb schools he sent me off to, long, long ago, was the fascinating clothes I got to see, and sometimes to wear. Everything else I was supposed to learn there I'd already learned from him.

Contents

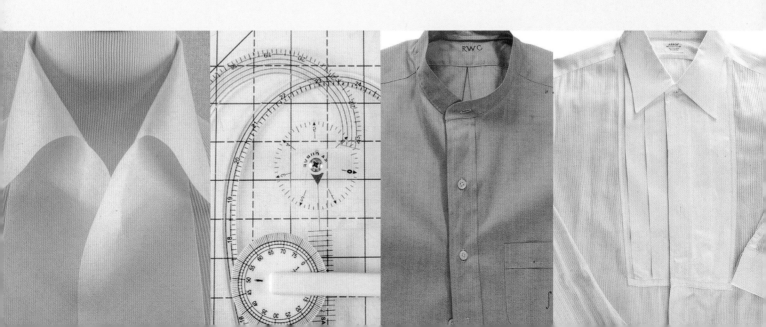

Introduction
Just one pattern!

When I first received the (somewhat staggering!) idea that I could possibly make some of my own clothes, my initial thought was, "Well, I'll only need one pattern for the shirt".

After all, it was clear even to a not-yet-maker that no matter the color, fabric, styles, or other specifics of any particular shirt, the shirts I already had were all fundamentally the same. And it was perfectly obvious that if I could learn to make one shirt, I'd be easily able to make others with different collars and other details, even different ways of fitting, not to mention different fabrics, without much or any changing of the basic, core patterns or processes.

Forty years of home sewing, a handful of sewing books and DVDs, and a thirty-year career in the how-to-sew industry has only reinforced the power and pertinence of this basic strategy, especially for this self-taught, nonprofessional garment-maker: learn how to do one basic thing reasonably well and you can mine the variations more or less endlessly. My efforts to do just that with shirt-like garments is what this book is all about, moving both myself and hopefully you, too, from shirtmaking to shirt designing.

My first sewing book, *Shirtmaking*, lays out how any motivated sewer can make dress shirts that reasonably approach top-quality custom-made garments. In the process of preparing that book I'd started to become fascinated with how deeply useful it was, in so many ways, to separate the aspects of a shirt—of any project, really—that could or should remain the same from those that could or might be varied. In other words, to see the core behind the details. And by the time I'd seen the book in print, this had become by far the most interesting aspect of my whole shirtmaking—indeed, any garment making—project: separating the core from the details on a range of arguably shirt-type garments, and exploring both core and details in depth, in order to expand our capacity to design and make shirt-like garments that are just what we happen to want at the time.

I made an effort to demonstrate this bringing together of core and detail in my first book, filling its last chapter on design options with examples of what I was currently doing with the dress-shirt skill set covered therein, which by then was anything but dress shirts. The garments at right, most made for inclusion in the first book, still make the point well, I think. Each of these was developed directly from my personal dress-shirt basic pattern (a somewhat moving target over the years, but in essentials, just one pattern), and none of its core pattern shapes was altered in any way that impacted the fit, except when the sleeve lengths and necklines needed to be adapted to the intended wearer.

What IS a Shirt?

Before we take another step, let me clarify what I'm regarding as a shirt for the purposes of this project. Any garment that hangs from the shoulders and has a neckline; has a mostly single-layer, mostly rectangular torso shaped, if at all, primarily by the shoulder and side seams; has no internal structure, padding, or interfacing except possibly in a collar or cuffs; and has sleeves that project from the body at an angle, rather than fall parallel to it, counts as a shirt here. Garments that match this feature list tend to fit quite simply whether snug or very loose, and to have finished seams because there are typically no linings. An aura of utility and humbleness colors the whole category, even if only as a memory of its simple beginnings; there aren't many more ancient or universal strategies for covering the upper human body. Exceptions, refinements, add-on details, and mergings with other garment types are all welcome, because the point here isn't to definitively declare what is or isn't a shirt, but to open up the category to facilitate seeing connections we might otherwise miss, and to encourage cross-fertilization.

Most broadly, I'll consider calling a shirt any garment that I can make in essentially the same way as I would make what the world would universally regard as a shirt. If I can make this (insert any plain old shirt you've made), well, then I guess I can also make… all these other things without learning any new stuff; and all THESE other things if I just learn THIS… etc.

Inspired by Clothes

When I decided to try to make a dress shirt, I simply wanted to make one just like the favorite shirts I already had. What I lacked in sewing knowledge I made up for with an enthusiast's appreciation for shirts themselves, in detail. Beyond the fabrics and colors, I was very conscious of, and critical about, two aspects of any shirt: The SHAPES of the pieces that made it up, and the exact details of the WAYS those pieces were assembled. With some minor differences,

These garments are photo-profiled online

Full-size printable patterns from these garments, details, or muslins are online.

From one basic dress shirt pattern, six completely different designs; details available in online content. Each one was created simply by swapping in new details and redrawing free edges as desired. No changes affected the fit of the basic pattern, except for the necklines and sleeve lengths on 2 and 3, which were altered to accommodate a female's proportions.

From top left to bottom right:

1. Pinpoint oxford dress shirt with neckband collar; this is my dress shirt pattern unaltered.
2. Silk pullover blouse with applied self-fabric pleat panel and collar band ready for separate collars; shown in the *Shirtmaking* book.
3. Linen pleated blouse with a one-piece bias-cut un-interfaced asymmetrical collar; shown on the cover of *Shirtmaking*.
4. Cotton pullover shirt with piped applied panels of Japanese fabric and cowboy shirt cuffs, featured in *Threads* issue 67.
5. Wool twill pullover shirt with silk-lined sleeves and cotton-faced collar, bib, hem, and yoke; shown in *Shirtmaking*.
6. Wool yoked jacket with machine-knitted cashmere sleeves and a fully lined and interlined body; shown in *Shirtmaking*.

all of my favorite shirts had very similar construction features, and I took these to be standard, essential to what made my shirts.

But with my very first commercial shirt pattern (a Vogue Designer pattern) I was shocked to discover that while my new pattern had the shapes I needed—or close enough—the ways it was showing me for putting them together were clearly nothing like the ways MY shirts had been put together. Yikes!

My purchased shirts were obviously manufactured, not home sewn, but until this moment I hadn't realized that these were such different worlds—and, I was to find out, by no means equally accessible. From that simple but stunning recognition evolved my Prime Directive as both a sewer and a writer about sewing: let's look first at similar clothes made by professionals whenever we're trying to make our own, and as much as possible let that experience inform how we use the home-sewing tools we have.

We won't always be able or willing to do exactly what the pros are doing, and we will certainly be able to improve on some manufacturing methods to better suit ourselves (no doubt, what we want to improve is often the clearest thing we do learn from clothes!). Still, I find that nothing takes me quicker to that wonderful "Okay, I'm going to make THAT!" moment, or serves me better on the way, than a close, inside-and-out look at some interestingly manufactured clothing. And if I want to figure out a detail, there's nothing better than having it in hand to examine. I'm unashamedly a "home" sewer and often awestruck by what my fellow home sewers are managing to create, but I always want to feel I'm as informed as possible about how things are done in the world of clothes makers who aren't pausing to think about how a home sewer might manage to do what they're making a living at. There are so many more of them than of us, after all, and they've been working at and thinking about the process in ways I can barely imagine, and for far longer! But neither do I want to have to buy a bunch of industrial equipment or train in a factory to get to make clothes I'll really enjoy, both during and after the sewing. That's why I'm always looking for that best-of-both-worlds middle ground and am open to any and all tricks, tools, and workarounds that can help me get there.

So, What's in This Book?

First, since there's such a remarkably wide range of diverse manufactured garments that share some basic, "core" features with what most would call "a shirt," we'll look at a bunch of these, both for their similarities and for their unique features, to see what we can borrow and learn. Second, it's easy to come up with a basic torso-fitting pattern for any arguably shirt-like garment, which is a simple rectangular body shape. And then it's easy to develop your own range of diverse garment projects by changing only the selection and shape of the details, such as the fabrics, findings, and finishes. So, we'll look at both these steps: pulling out basic patterns, and adding new details.

In chapter 1, we'll explore where and how to get these basic patterns—which from here on out I'll call blocks, to borrow a manufacturer's term. In the last chapters (3 through 7), we'll examine details and specialized techniques associated with each of five general block types into which I find it useful to divvy up the Shirt Universe, as in the diagrams at right. And in between, in chapter 2, we'll review a few key generic construction techniques in common use among professional makers of all kinds of shirts, so we can bring our blocks and details together. To really get rolling we need patterns, and these this workbook also provides: a large collection of full-size add-on detail patterns in digital, printable format, with a heavy emphasis on collars and center-front openings, the easiest areas in which to bring variety to basic block patterns.

Within each chapter, you'll also find a Resources section and further reading suggestions appropriate to the styles or information collected there, as well as a few additional ideas under the heading "To Consider." I hope you will!

In my previous life as a *Threads* editor and currently in support of this project, I've had the pleasure of connecting with many fascinating and knowledgeable sewers, designers, makers, and experts, so you'll find example garments from, and features by and about, some of these folk scattered about these pages. Many thanks to all my contributors for their generosity!

Finally, what's NOT in this book? This is a design book, not primarily a sewing how-to, nor is it a project reference in the sense of providing start-to-finish directions for any particular garment. Rather, it's my effort to adapt this mostly professionally oriented information into something more flexible, more comfortable, and more fun for home sewers to enjoy playing with.

Five Block Types

Here are my five general shirt block types, showing typical shapes and pieces. Many variations are of course possible.

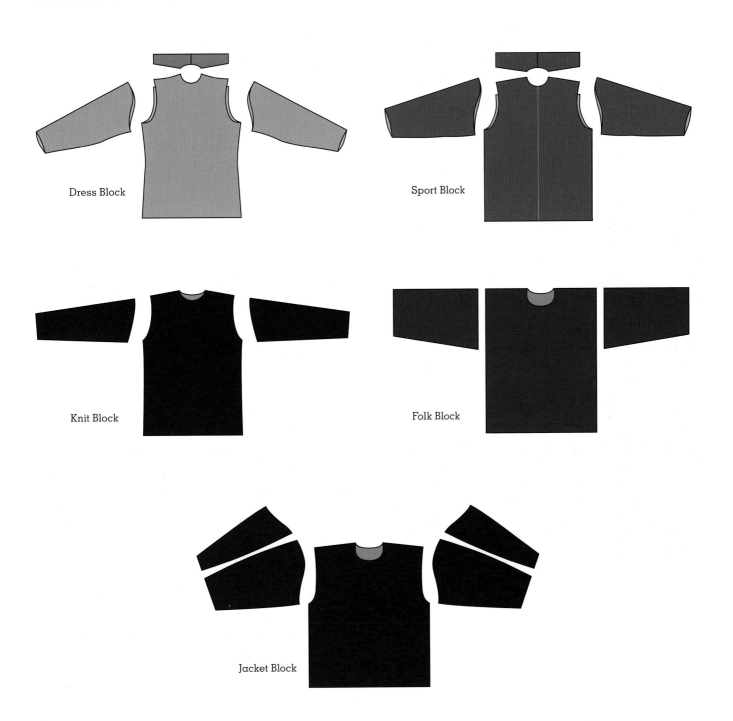

Dress Block

Sport Block

Knit Block

Folk Block

Jacket Block

Despite offering observations and processes on the all-important subject of fitting, this isn't a fitting book either. What is here is limited to fitting my own quirky (but by no means unique) figure. Happily, many experts have chosen to dwell on fitting, offering books, videos, and workshops that are a truly marvelous resource, and I list a few in chapter 1.

But if you're one for whom all DIY/how-to fitting solutions have failed, here's my fervent advice: find a local expert fitter and pay him or her to solve it for you, one on one and in person! Any competent dressmaker, tailor, or theatrical costumer (and obviously any custom shirtmaker, local, visitable, or online) is worth asking what they'd charge to help you out. If fitting has you stalled out and broken down on your road to really enjoying sewing and design, then this is no time to refuse to go to a mechanic.

Digital and Online Content

In order to provide the patterns here both full size and printable, there's a significant online component to this book, described with full access instructions at www.creativepub.com/pages/shirtmaking-workbook. You'll also find online larger versions of many photos in the book, expanded photo collections, and quite a bit of additional content beyond what it makes sense to print; look for the icons shown below. Also, I've collected a truly vast pile of links while "working" on this project—suppliers, inspiration, tutorials, bloggers, books, and more—which I'm happy to share online as well.

 These garments are photo-profiled online

 Full-size printable patterns from these garments, details, or muslins are online.

📖 Online article

You're also invited to follow my blog created for readers of this book, in which I'll be posting on related topics, continuing my explorations started here, profiling additional garment finds, digging deeper with my contributors and other experts, and of most interest to me, offering a series of detailed, step-by-step garment sew-alongs. These document garment projects derived from the patterns and ideas supplied in these pages, freeing me from many space, schedule, and size constraints compared to print, and allowing for both real-time and archivable comments and questions. Books must end, but blogs?

One of the biggest pleasures I've had in this *Shirtmaking Workbook* project has been the excuse it provided to indulge in "research shopping" as I collected garments to profile and dissect for each of my block chapters. Naturally, there are many more garments out there I'd still like to get my greedy hands and camera on, and even more wonderful and intriguing pieces that would presumably never become available to beg, borrow, or buy. It's my fond hope that one or another of the digital addresses I've created or could create (Pinterest? Flickr? The blog?) will become a space where other folks with cool, treasured, and exceptional garments will consider posting detailed photographic "profiles," similar at least in the level of detail I've tried to maintain in this book with my own haul. And of course, it'll be wonderful to have galleries available for readers to post, describe, and ask about their own creations … oh, the possibilities!

Who Is This Book For?

This book is not what I'd call an advanced text, but it doesn't start at the absolute beginning either. It assumes some basic experience with garment sewing, with altering conventional sewing patterns, with the machines and tools for those activities, and if no experience at least a willingness to get involved with pattern design. Ideally, the reader will have made some sort of shirt at least once before, and maybe even read my previous book on the subject. But any determined and fearless beginning sewer can be "ready" for this book, along with help from others, and online.

Nonetheless, familiarity with, or access to, my first shirtmaking book isn't essential to using this book. The earlier book contains complete details on dress-shirt construction and custom fitting. Techniques in it will naturally be referenced here now and again, but every effort has been made not to duplicate techniques and information already provided in the first work. Nor is this a book about sewing or designing just for men, despite what many folks will assume simply from the word "shirt" being in the title. This is a book for anyone who's ever worn a shirt and would like to make one, regardless of gender. The techniques here will enable anyone with access to a physical garment to copy it quite accurately.

Finally, the project that launched me into this book was and remains focused on everyday, utility clothing. I'm interested in making my own garment sewing both more efficient and more adventurous—quick to make but not boring to wear, with cool shapes and details—so I'm particularly drawn to simple garments and toward simplifying any inspiring clothes I see down to their most essential elements and most provocative details. I hope nonetheless that readers will feel the ideas and observations I've assembled here will assist them in going in any direction with their own new garment projects. Most of all, I truly hope you'll find the same pleasure in exploring shirt design as I have, to even a small degree. And as always, if you discover anything really neat, by all means share it with the rest of us!

My blog at www.shirtmakingwithdpc.com is always open.

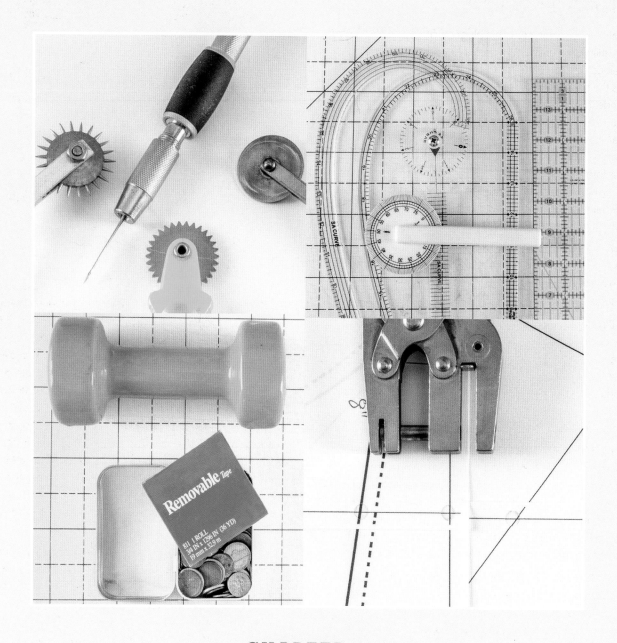

CHAPTER 1

Block Logic

What Is a Block?

Within the garment industry, a block is a fit-adjusted but detail-free, utility garment pattern used as the starting point for creating detail-rich fashion patterns with the same underlying shape and fit as the block. It has no features or parts that would be likely to change from garment to garment or season to season, so for my purposes here, it would be the core of an entire shirt, without the details. A block records the fit, silhouette, and ease of a specific garment style adapted to a specific body, list of measurements, or dress form, ensuring that a trademark fit and feel remains the same across a collection of similar garments. A manufacturer starts with a tried-and-true block for each style, because it's more efficient to build on pattern development they've already done.

As you've no doubt noticed, this is exactly the logic behind my use of a single dress shirt pattern—my personal block—to generate each of the quite different garments in the introduction. And it's the logic behind all that follows in this book.

My Big Idea is simply that we sewers working outside the garment industry can also make practical use of the block concept whenever it suits us, by developing a collection of personal blocks. From here on out, I'll be discussing blocks as personal tools keyed to and perfected for one person as opposed to the industrial tool, which is averaged to an entire population keeping it applicable to as many bodies as possible.

So, the First Really Great Thing about having a personal block (or several, to cover all the basic garment types you'd like to make more than once) is that you can use it to transfer your personal fit preferences to every future garment you make of that type, with little or no further adjustment or fit testing. Add different details and stylings to the block, and you'll have created a new design that fits like the original source for the block but has a new look.

A pared-down shirt block would thus consist only of the front, the back, and the sleeve—and the yoke if the original had one—but no specific collars, pockets, plackets, closures, cuffs or any other add-ons to or restylings of the basic shapes, as shown. You set aside all the attached fashion details and use just the body parts and the sleeve, ignoring any cut-on details or non-core shaping on those pieces you won't want to have as part of every future garment you design from the block, such as any pleats or tucks whose exact location is not essential to the fit and could thus be placed differently or converted into ease or gathers, or the hem shapes, or however the center-front closure is handled on the fashion pattern.

Shirt Block Categories

The Second Really Great Thing I find in the block concept for home-based garment makers is how it encourages a liberating and design-friendly sort of modular thinking. We begin to think about all that could be done with a single block, and from there we ask what other block(s) it might be good to have, in order to do things that wouldn't work so well with the first one. Design starts looking more like an endlessly open game with recombinant elements, and not so much a waiting for the perfect idea to appear fully formed either in your mind's eye or in a pattern company or ready-to-wear (RTW) catalog. It's certainly true that any really successful garment is a synergy beyond its collected features, but the features are there nonetheless, and anything that helps you move them around more freely, or see them more distinctly, is a plus for designing, I believe. So the block idea is as much an aid to creativity as it is an aid to fit.

As I mentioned in the introduction and explore in separate chapters that follow, the Shirt Universe seems to me to break down into at least five useful categories, for each of which a distinct fitting block might be good to have: A Dress (or shaped) Block, a Sport (or loose-fit) Block, a Knit (or stretchy) Block, a Folk (or pure rectangular) Block, and a Shirt-Jacket (or oversized) Block. Thus separated out, I'm encouraged not only to think about all the interesting details that naturally go with each block's native style, but also how details that might have seemed tied to a particular category might just as fruitfully shift around between categories—how a jacket collar, for instance, might be really interesting as a sport-shirt collar, too.

There's nothing ultimate about my categories, and lots of other just as helpful and perhaps more useful to you ways to slice up the same universe. These categories of mine are chiefly the way I find it most productive to organize my explorations for this specific project, and if they inspire you to come up with different categories, or to forget about making categories altogether, I'd call that useful in itself. Certainly there are plenty of shirt-related garments, styles, and patterns—and possible shirt blocks—that don't easily fit into one or any of my five categories, or could fit in more than one. Block logic remains the same however you apply the concept, and to whatever extent you do so.

Where to Get Your Block(s)

Besides adding style, ease, and shaping to a basic fitted shell pattern—in other words, designing from scratch—you can also start with any styled pattern that's already well fitted to your body, removing non-core features and details to pare it down to its essential shape and fit. This is similar to the process you might go through to test the fit of a styled pattern in muslin, for which you'd also remove details, but it might include some that you also wanted to test, such as the scale or shape of a collar. A block could also be thought of as simply the record of the muslin after all the adjustments and tests are complete. If you've ever made up a pattern more than once with any changes beyond a different fabric, you're already using it as a block. Naturally, you'd be wise to choose as basic a fashion pattern as you can find if your goal is a block with maximum potential for adding variety to later, but it's important to note that any pattern with a neckline and armholes could be treated as a shirt block. As you trace it, you can retain as many unique details as you'd like to repeat on future garments. It's just that as a pattern increases in complexity, it also becomes more complicated to alter it, which, after all, is the point of making a block in the first place—it is not an end in itself but a starting point for something new.

Once you have a block, there's a hierarchy to its parts based on which are easier or safer to change and which you might want to just develop a new block for—it's a sort of high-to-low order of coreness, if you will. It starts at the top, as shown with red lines (above, top), with the shoulders, and moves down the sides to the armhole and sleeve cap; getting all those right and then not messing with them is really the most important thing your block is giving you. Continuing down the sides, the overall width of the body pieces—or in other words, the placement of the side seams in relation to the armhole and shoulders, and covering you at the widest—is next in the "don't touch!" ranking.

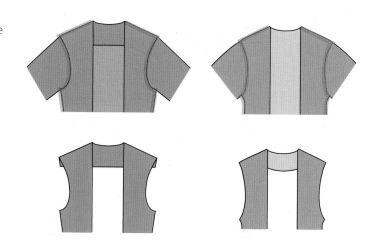

The shaping and length of the hem; the amount of flare, taper, or waist suppression at the sides (within limits going inward, of course); and the shape of the sleeves as determined by the underarm seams lines are all safe to reimagine. Then it's back to the top center for the easiest part of the block to change at will: the neckline, and by sheer proximity, the center-front as well. How you like a necktie or buttoned collar to fit will give you the no-tighter-than-this limit for the neck, but moving outward and up or down—well, that's where all the fun is, as far as I'm concerned.

Blocks within Blocks

Consider also that you can apply the block concept to portions of a favorite pattern by converting some of it into a more basic, and thus more flexible, shape, or by isolating some already basic portion of it for use elsewhere. Necklines are again a likely target for these ideas. Simply by redrawing or tracing to bring a nonstandard neckline back to the shape of your basic shirt block's neckline, you can from then on apply any sort of collar to it as you'd be able to apply to a conventional shirt, as in the green example in the diagram on page 13, and having a basic neckline in place would be a good, square-one starting point for adding any other type of collar or neckline.

You only need a portion of a block to explore an isolated area of it. As indicated in the lower half of the diagram above, all the high-order parts of a shirt block can be captured with nothing more than the partial pieces shown, which leads directly to the process I used throughout this book to explore different collar and center-front design details.

Three Kinds of Sub-Block

1. Shoulder and Armscye

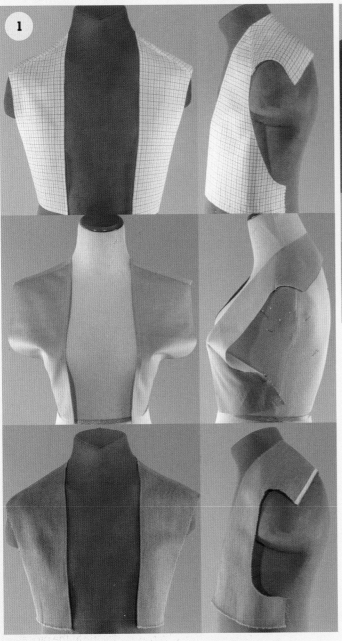

2. Center-Front and Neckline

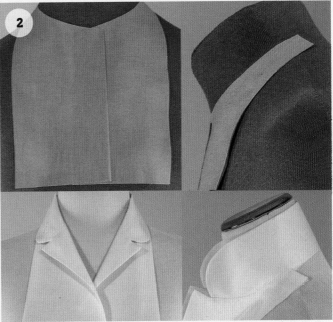

1 The three **shoulder and armscye** sub-blocks at left contain the minimum needed parts and edges to represent a full garment block when testing out a collar or CF design on a form or body, and then to transfer the test to the full block. Note the bottom one has a slightly wider neckline than the top one; it's from a Jacket block, while the top one is from a Sport block. The middle example shows that only the top of the armscye is really needed or otherwise the sub would be unnecessarily wide.

2 A **center-front and neckline** sub-block goes under the above sub-block, and needs only to extend beyond the shoulder seam in back and as far down in front as the opening needs to be tested. Most collars only need to be adjusted at the center back to fit as wanted.

3. Full Neckline

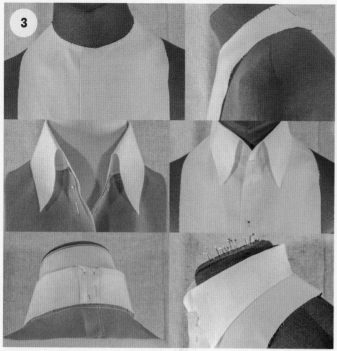

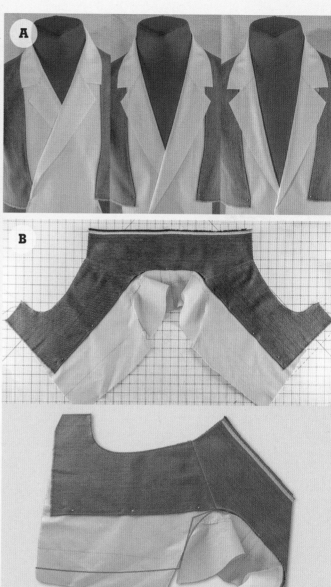

3 A **full-neckline** sub-block does allow a collar to be joined all around, which simplifies open-collar testing, and allows it to be placed over a draped collar to transfer its neckline to it.

A The grain of a **CF&N** module can be shifted during draping since it will be simply traced around when merged with the final on-grain pattern.

B Off the form, the **S&A** lays flat for easy alignment with the full front block pattern, as will the parts of the collar and CF test, which can be dissembled for tracing separately if they've been altered during the test.

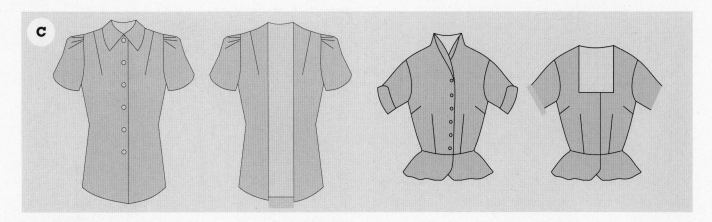

C For each new collar, CF, or neckline I wanted to try out for this book, I isolated just the neckline and a short length of center-front, adding the collar to a dickie or bib-shaped scrap, as shown as shown on page 15 (2). This scrap, a center-front & neckline sub-block, is cut as needed with no back, but only the neckline front shape and CF overlap I want to use with whatever collar shape I'm testing. Then it's matched on the form or body with what I've called here a shoulder and armscye sub-block to easily connect it to whatever shirt block I want. A center-front and neckline sub-block can be as easily dropped into and then blended with pretty much any top pattern to which I want to add a different CF or collar without converting them to blocks, just removing the same area on the pattern as shown above (6), either all the way to the hem or bust or other level as appropriate.

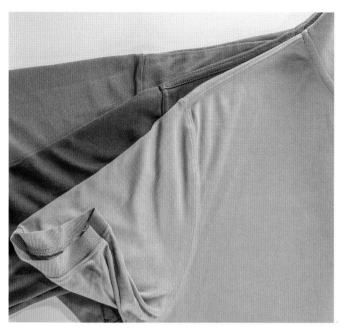

Any collar itself can be treated as a sub- or mini-block simply by considering as its core the seams that connect to other pieces (neckline or collar stand) and its details as all the free edges, as shown above.

Taken together, these blocks-within-blocks ideas are behind most of the design ideas in this book. Mini-blocks are thus my choice for the Third Really Great Thing to come from the block concept.

Fitting

Making a block from an existing pattern seems like the most approachable route for the sewer at home to follow, and I definitely recommend it. But what if you don't have a pattern that you like well enough to convert into a block? Here are the options I see:

- Buy a better pattern.
- Take a class on pattern adjusting, preferably in person.
- Buy a custom pattern or shirt from a fitting professional.
- Draft a pattern using your measurements.
- Drape a basic shirt body.
- Copy an existing garment.

The Resources for this chapter (see page 30) can get you started on the first three. I'll look at the last three in more detail, but first let's examine fit in more detail.

How Should a Shirt Fit?

It's easy enough to spell out the critical fitting points for a shirt (shoulders, neck, wrists, chest, waist, and hem) and to declare that each should be just big enough but never too big, and positioned just so, never too long or too short, as appropriate for each block style. But to do so suggests that there's only one combination of dimensions that will fill the bill for each of us, which is clearly not so. Take a look at these three polo shirts from my closet above, each of which I wear with pleasure, with no sense that one fits better than the others or suits some different purpose or activity. Certainly I notice the difference when I put each one on—I even enjoy it—but decreasingly so as the day wears on; they all quickly just feel right.

So, the question of what's the "right" fit for any particular shirt type is subjective, complex, and quite intriguing. We're very deeply trained to expect that shirts will fit us and others as they already do, which is quite haphazardly, given how far from average many of us are. Yet average Small, Medium, and Large dimension charts are all that's behind 99 percent of the world's shirts. Very few shirts out there are fitted perfectly, yet most of them are regarded as working fine and looking perfectly good.

If you were to select a handful of your different kinds of shirts that you really like to wear, and then could magically remake each of the shirts so they all fit to the same custom standard at each critical point, do you think that in every case, your shirts or their look would be improved? My answer would definitely be "Not always!" Sometimes, NOT fitting just the right way is a big part of what makes a look or a good-feeling garment work.

Shoulder fit demonstrates this fit/don't-fit question well. When you select a S-M-L shirt, you're typically going to choose by the chest measurement, and you'll have to put up with whatever neck, sleeves, and shoulders are going to come along. So if your shoulders are narrower, or your torso circumference bigger (at the chest, waist, or both) than the average determined by the manufacturer, the shirt shoulders are going to fall off the ends of your actual shoulders. And if you buy larger just to get your sleeves long enough, the problem's amplified. It's a very common sight, and it produces a look and feel that many simply experience as normal, especially if it's part of almost every shirt they own.

A customized pattern or garment, on the other hand, is typically going to start with fitted shoulders and adjust everything else as needed, resulting in a strikingly different look and feel. There's no question which result is, the better-fitting one. But is it always the preferable one? To my eye, fitting or not fitting are simply distinct style options, and if you like them both, you might want to have blocks reflecting them both.

Measuring Your Clothes

The best way I know of to begin turning the complexities into practical action is to start measuring your own clothes and keeping a record of the results. After all, the fitting question is just about what measurements equal what sort of fit and what kind of look. We're all experts at which of our clothes feel best, but do we know what measurements those have? At right are some example measurings in my files for favorite shirts, a quick photo being an ideal way to keep the records together with the garments.

At the same time, I suggest making it a point to try on more clothes that aren't yours! (When shopping, visiting, stopping to chat … seriously! Carry a tape and camera.) I have discovered that what my usual clothes feel like isn't always what I might prefer, but I never knew otherwise because I stick so thoughtlessly to what I'm used to.

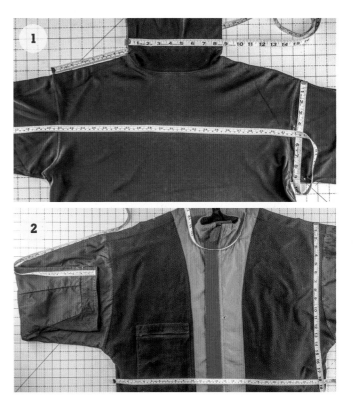

Drafting

There are multiple methods for drafting your own patterns or blocks from either standardized or personal measurements, using current and vintage pattern-drafting texts. There is also specialized pattern-drafting software, and you can even do it for free online or in a general-purpose vector graphics program such as Adobe Illustrator (see Resources). In any of these approaches, the process is quite fascinating but labor-intensive, and their various learning curves are not trivial, especially with the old drafts that are filled with jargon, odd phrasings, and references to knowledge assumed but unspecified. However, there are lots of very enticing designs available to those willing to take it up, especially for vintage-fashion enthusiasts. In its several modern incarnations, it's the foundation step for further pattern development and design using paper, pencils, curves, and rulers, commonly called flat-pattern design.

In essence, drafting involves inserting specific body measurements into a long series of formulas, or some kind of software interface, for plotting points at precise distances from previous points, as in the example on page 20. When all the points are plotted, you or the software will connect the dots to create the pattern outline for the main body pattern pieces, by now scaled to the measurements inserted. This may be all you need, but the process typically assumes that the results will be further refined with adjustments to a trial garment made from the draft, because

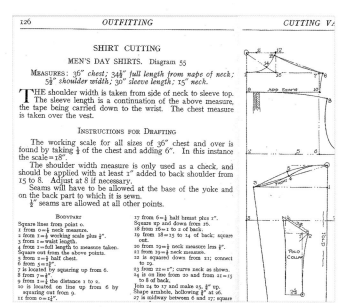

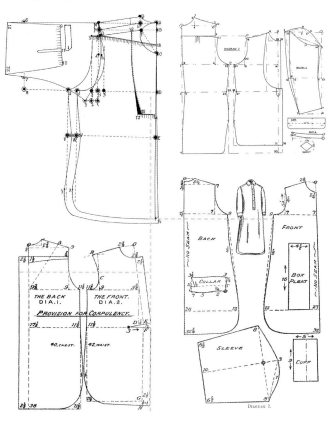

the measurements alone aren't usually sufficient to capture all the oddities of posture and angle needed for the final pattern. If there are no such oddities, a draft can be a great path to a custom shirt pattern or block, and even if there are, it's a very good start. But also be aware that any draft is a specific style incorporating someone else's decisions about how much fashion and wearing ease should go where, and exactly what shapes every piece should have. So you'll have to make it to know how it's going to look, and what else it will need to really fit.

Besides the free online drafts, which are a wonderful quick source for rudimentary but still customized basic shirt-pattern shapes, the main value of drafting is simply the ability to see and compare the shapes in the many and various "here's-what-you're-drafting" diagrams they all provide. After looking at a half-dozen basic shirt-draft diagrams, as you can easily do online, and in the several further examples I've provided at right, you could easily alter any existing patterns to be more like the shape in a given draft, simply by redrawing on top of the skeleton, or core, provided by your existing pattern, without an elaborate point-plotting system.

Draping

If drafting is the geometer's path to pattern design and adjustment, then draping is the sculptor's, because it skips all the rulers, measuring, and paper and pencils, and goes right to manipulating the fabric on a body or a dress form. Even though it's typically associated with soft, flowing ("drapey") fabrics, draping can also be used to create precise and restrained shapes in crisp fabrics, all while adapting them to a specific body in an immediate and

intuitive way. Subsequent testing with a mock-up garment is still required, because drapes are just pinned-together mock-ups. But tweaks are likely to be less than with drafting, because draping is testing-on-the-body and pattern-making all at once and captures much that pure measurement will miss. In a very real way, any type of fitting directly on the body is a type of draping, so there's no reason to regard it as an exotic practice.

I have provided a complete process for what you might call semi-draping a dress-shirt block in my earlier book, "semi" in the sense that you start with an existing shirt pattern with a yoke that matches your shoulder measurements. To summarize it here, you smooth out and pin the prefab yoke in muslin exactly as wanted to a tight T-shirt you're wearing, then drape fabric rectangles smoothly and grain straight over the front and back, tracing the yoke outlines underneath onto the overlays to capture exactly how the fronts and back will join the yoke to reproduce the drape. You go back to the pattern for the sleeves and armholes, which connect at the yoke ends. (If you're very little different on the right side than on the left, you could drape on just one side.) It's actually quite doable to drape like this on yourself, especially if you can get just a little help marking the back—getting together with sewing friends for a drape-fest is of course a good idea, but best of all, I think, is to work on a customized body form (see Don't Fit Yourself Alone!, page 25), as I'm doing in the photos, above.

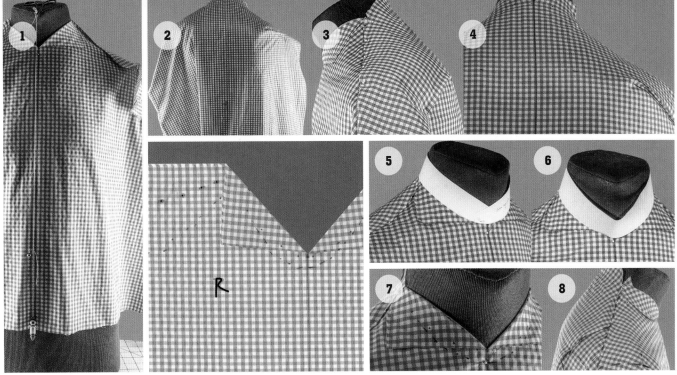

Draping a fitted shirt on a custom form.

If you don't have a custom form, work with a sewing friend, draping each other while wearing tight knit tops to pin into. Working on a standard form isn't helpful unless you're draping for standard sizes.

1 Mark center lines on two rectangles of woven gingham about 24 inches (61 cm) long and plenty wider than your form/figure. Slash about 3 inches (7.5 cm) in on the line for the front piece and pin it as shown, slightly above the natural neckline with the top edges covering the shoulders. Adjust each upper corner so the grain is square to a plumb line at center.

2 Center, pin, and square the other piece as shown above the natural neckline in back, clipping the center as needed at the neck edge. Fold out and pin horizontal darts from any natural peaks as shown so the grain returns to horizontal across the back.

3 Fold under and pin to create visually matching front-yoke edges from neck to arm, slightly in front of the natural shoulder line on both sides.

4 Fold under the back side darts to create matching back edges for the yoke, tracing across a plaid strip to keep the darts and yoke edge in a straight line as much as possible. Mark the sides of each back dart fold; these will become shaped seams when the yoke and back shapes are traced and separated.

5, 6 & 7 Place paper-strip versions of collar bands in whatever shape you want to create necklines for over the drape, and trace along their lower edges when they are positioned as wanted to mark the necklines, as shown at (7). I also liked the shape that the simply folded-back triangles created, so I marked those folds, too. (As shown in the photo to the left of 7.)

8 Before I removed the two draped rectangles, I folded them in a different way to create a no-yoke pattern marked in red, inspired by the Pointer Coat (see page 113).

In these photos I'm working without a preexisting yoke, generating a draped one as I go (and resulting in an asymmetrical yoke, which the earlier method avoids, if the yoke is narrow front to back), or in the latter shots, exploring a design without a yoke. I'm still relying on plugged-in sleeves and armholes from existing patterns.

The main disadvantage I see in these drape methods is that it's easy to over-fit, but that's easy enough to spot and correct for in the muslin test; in my case, it's usually just a matter of slightly relaxing the curves going into the yoke as they approach the sleeves. Symmetry doesn't come naturally to the draping process, which I find much easier to do across the full form rather than just on one side, but if you want truly customized results I think there's no better way to go. And for the best of both flat-patterning and draping, I refer you to my semi-drape method as an excellent way to add draped shoulders to an otherwise plotted-out pattern, whether you arrive at that by drafting or from a commercial pattern. Next is my favorite method of all …

Copying a Shirt 📖

There's one serious downside of all of the approaches so far covered: you have to both create (or buy, or alter) the pattern and then make it up in order to try it out with a wearable test garment. Unless you're very experienced, there's really no other way to know what you've got.

But because we're dealing with shirts, which offer nothing like the fitting challenges of, say, pants, form-fitted bodices, or shaped tailoring, there's another very powerful option, and that's to seek out an already existing shirt, new or old, bought or borrowed, that you like to wear or are at least okay with wearing and to copy it.

Copying is quite easy to do and doesn't hurt the shirt, so you don't need to own it, or even to particularly like any other aspect of it, so long as your shirt falls reasonably smoothly over your shoulders in a way you like and feels good at the armholes. As discussed previously, it's up to you whether or not the shoulders are the "right" length. Any other fitting issues you might have with it, such as sleeves not the right length, neckline, collar or cuffs not

comfortable or close enough, chest or waist circumference not right, are easy to change by basic lengthening or shortening and/or a simple redrawing the seam lines. Altering the fit at the shoulders and underarms is a bit trickier than are any of these other fixes, so those are the parts you'll be better off copying. And if you DO see that you'll need to tweak the shoulders further, usually because of a shoulder slope issue (drooping plaids or other horizontals are a clear tip-off), even if the shirt is in a soft draping fabric that smooths out on its own wrinkles or drag lines that would otherwise point to problems, as shown above, you can certainly do a semi-drape to fix that using your copy as the starting pattern. This is my current, best of all worlds, process.

To make an accurate outline of all the major pieces of any typical shirt, set up a large pinnable board like cardboard or foam core on a big flat surface, cover it with paper, then arrange the shirt over it, sequentially laying out each shirt piece (half-front, half-back, half-sleeve, half-yoke) completely flat, with no concern for how the other pieces need to lay to allow this, so you can see every seam and edge completely all around without distorting the piece to be copied. Pin the layers through to the board in a few places to keep them from shifting. Next, push a pin through all layers multiple times as you run the pin along each seam or edge, leaving behind a series of pinholes on the paper that you can later connect with a pencil, creating the outline of the copied piece. Place more holes closer together on tighter curves than gentler ones, and only one at each end of straight lines, since you'll connect these with a ruler and don't need to follow any tiny inaccuracies from the pinned fabric.

The tools for copying a shirt include, from the bottom:

A A large sheet of cardboard or foam core or even a folded blanket that you can push a pin into.

B Large sheets of thin paper, taped together if needed to be big enough. (I order gridded flip-chart paper from Amazon for these; it stores easily and ships in a large flat cardboard box, ideal for A.)

C Pencil, eraser, colored markers, a few curves, and a transparent ruler for drawing and truing the lines between the pinholes.

D A straightedge ideally as long as the garment for laying against garment sections you know to be straight, such as the center-front closure's edge and the fold of the sleeve.

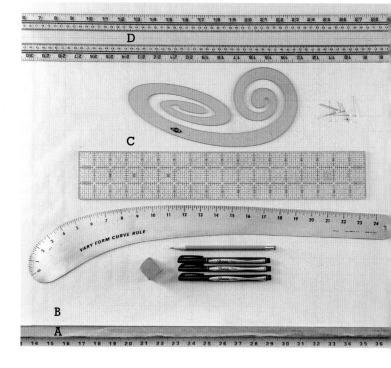

1 Front and **back.** Lay the long straightedge against the CF closure edge as you're arranging the front, and pin that first to help ensure that the rest of the piece is lying as cut. In back, do the same with the center-back (CB), which you can locate by folding the hem and the yoke in half. Fold out any back pleats as shown (estimate gathered amount by spreading the back just below them) from the top to the hem, and note the depth so you can put this extra wearing ease back in anywhere, and in any way you like on future garments. You don't need the exact hem curve because you can easily redraw this to suit as you trace off future unique patterns from the block.

2 Yoke and **sleeve.** First pin these against a ruler as shown to set the alignment of each full piece. Mark the mid-yoke by folding it in half. The hidden half of the sleeve seam may be a different curve, so feel through the layers and pin along both the visible seam and the one out of sight below, noting on the paper which sleeve side is facing up. Note that the cuff keeps the sleeve end from being fully flattened, but the fold will remain a straight line, and the seam curve will also extend smoothly, so all you need at this end is the total length along the fold to the cuff. The cuff's length and width can be simply measured; for the block it's just a rectangle, not shaped in any way.

3 Pin down the **collar** and **stand** each on its own, because they are probably joined with two different curves and these would be lost if both were forced to lie flat at the same time, even if it appears easy to do so. As with all the other pieces, you only need half, so fold to find the midpoints. As you move from piece to piece, shift the paper or use a new sheet so you don't get confused. Your final outlines will be without seam allowances, ideal for tracing and just what you want for a block. There's a video of the complete process at my website, www.shirtmakingwithdpc.com, and more details on refining the outlines coming right up.

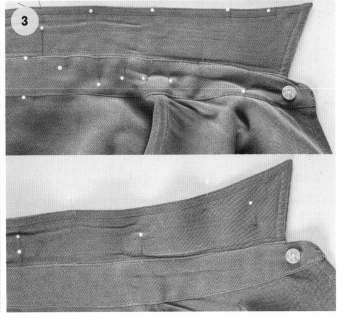

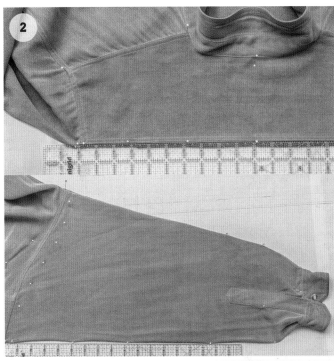

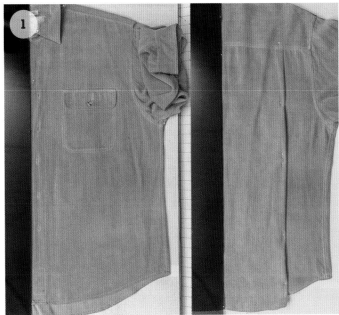

General Pattern Skills

It's my opinion that plain old drawing is at the heart of pattern design, which I find both liberating and clarifying. These specific drawing skills are about seeing and laying out outlines in just the right shape for pieces that will wrap a three-dimensional figure in a way that you want. I think there's no question this is a skill anyone can develop. Go back to the shirt draft examples on page 20 and see if it doesn't seem easy to imagine redrawing some or even all of the edges on a draft diagram to make them more to your taste. This requires no additional drafting steps or formulas—just an idea, an eye, a pencil, and knowing which edges to leave alone (the connecting—core—ones) or to change equally. If you could do it on the diagram, you could do it to the full-size draft, too, or to any pattern.

The key difference between a well-drawn collection of pattern shapes and a true, working pattern is that the pattern comes after the pattern-play and fitting adjustments, and has all the kinks worked out along every seam and cutting line so that the finalized shapes will fit to each other when sewn. This requires an understanding of just how all the seams will be sewn, so you need to plan for any kind of seam allowance while you're getting the seam lines in shape, a process called truing, which is covered in most basic sewing texts. Ideally, this is the process of working out in your own mind exactly what you'll do at every step of the construction process, and doing that while you're finalizing the pattern to suit those steps, not as you're sewing.

To make it easiest to bring block and detail patterns together, and to redraw them, I prefer to have them all be without seam allowances until I'm ready to cut so I never have to wonder about them until then. I can then join and overlap things directly on their outlines, and draw new ones with no confusion about where to put them. If that idea drives you crazy, by all means do it your way, but remember that unless otherwise noted, all the patterns here, and all my diagrams on pattern usage, are without seam allowances.

Tools

The tools you'll need are all about drawing, cutting what you've drawn, and joining them to other drawings. Besides those shown at right, the rulers, curves, pencils, and markers already given for garment copying on page 22 are all on the list, as are scissors and rotary cutters for paper, tape (I like the Scotch removable kind, so I can change my mind without tearing anything), and a tape measure.

If you're interested in drafting, especially from vintage instructions, you'll benefit from having a tailor's square, which is assumed to be in your hands by all the old drafts. It gives you right angles, of course, so you can easily "square" a perpendicular line away from any other line. It also includes proportional scales at top right, so you can quickly find half or a quarter, or even a sixth, a third, or a twelfth of some given length right on the ruler. These are just the sort of lengths the drafts will call for, as you saw in the example on page 20 (top).

I'm a great fan of curves (they look so cool!) and you'll need at least a few of these too: a long slow one (get the metal one in the copying tools picture if you're getting only one) and a shorter quick one (as in the same image). There's no magic skill needed: they're just bent rulers with asymmetrical, ever-changing curves, so your chances are good of finding sections along the ruler that match the curve you want to smooth or redraw. Typically, you have to do this in sections because it's unlikely that any part of the ruler is exactly like the entire curve you want, unless it's quite a short one. Curves for clothing are made knowing that you need to draw armholes, necklines, and hips, so they're optimized for matching those sorts of shapes in few sections. The only trick is joining the sections smoothly as you slide the curve over your rough lines looking for a new match.

From top: The proportional scales on a tailor's square. SA curves and rolling rulers, a great help for all pattern drafting and seam allowance tru-ing. A pin vise for holding the tracing pin during long sessions of pin copy-ing. Weights, including a mint tin filled with coins, and removable tape. A standard hole punch for easiest ever alignment of tiled pdf patterns.

Forms

Don't Fit Yourself Alone!

Whatever route you take to a fitted basic pattern, here's my next bit of fitting advice, get a cus-tomized, full-size, three-dimensional fitting form; an upper-body double; or as I called it in my most popular ever *Threads* magazine article, a body CLONE. Trust me, this will be your best ever, always available, never-asleep fitting as-sistant and "how-does-this-actually-look?" consultant. Here's mine above. A cast body form such as this, created by wrap-ping one's own body in plaster, duct tape, or something similar, to extract its exact contours, asymmetries, posture, and angles, has been without question the most significant aid to my own fitting and design efforts. Once you get over the inevitable shock of seeing your own shape as others do, the benefits of working directly on "yourself" will amaze you.

And as for stepping back to really see how a detail you're thinking to add to your block will look, there's nothing bet-ter. It's exactly what I'll be using to display the detail patterns in the following pages. The form I use started with a plaster bandage cast filled with self-hardening foam, and it's still serving me well after nearly twenty years. Check out the whole article, complete with various methods for making your own form, and current sources on my blog.

Digital Tools

In my small work area, my sewing space is just a chair-spin away from my computer space, which pretty much always has Adobe Photoshop and Illustrator up and running. Plugged into it are currently three printers and a card reader for my camera. The newest of these printers has changed completely how I do pattern making, design, alterations, truing, and more. That's because it's also a scanner, and it both scans and prints up to 11 x 17 inches (28 x 43 cm)—fast! (Actually, it'll print to 13 x 19 inches [33 x 48 cm] and it cost less than $200—see details in Resources.) So the process of scanning in a full-size pattern or printing one out and taping

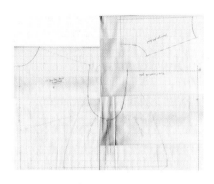

it together is simply NOT a drag; it's actually kinda fun.

What I'm most likely to scan these days are pinned copies from garments, which I can typically fit onto one or both sides of a 27 x 30-inch (69 x 76 cm) sheet of flip chart paper. I can then usually capture the best parts of these in four to six full-glass scans. Photoshop easily merges these files into a single large image, above, which then drops neatly into Illustrator perfectly to original scale, where it's literally a matter of seconds to click around the tracings, overlaying my connect-the-dots pencil lines with a perfect digital line, ripe for further play, as shown below.

Besides the one-click seam allowances (or seam lines if your source has only a cutting line), instant line-quality variations (colors, weights, dashes) and instant length readouts to any decimal accuracy of any line or line segment, straight or curved, the best bits for me are how easy it is to alter outlines in precise ways, and to overlay different transparent outlines for easy comparison, merging, and alignment.

I copied the shirt in these examples because I liked its loose, wide-shoulder fit, but also wanted to see how it would do with more fitted and more sloping shoulders, and thus hopefully have less of the plaid droop you can see on page 22. As shown below, here's what I did to achieve that easily in Illustrator: I copied all the outlines for the front, back, and yoke onto a new layer, locking the originals; generated a width guideline (the purple lines in the illustration) half the shoulder width I wanted in back and dragged copies of it perpendicular to the center-backs on the yoke and the back; and selected all the lines and end points along the armhole and side seams on the yoke and back and dragged them to hit the purple width guide with a vertical restraint (by holding the Shift key while dragging). The back and yoke width were now done. The front needed to be slightly less wide to match the yoke front edge, so I repeated everything there with a shorter width guideline. The front width was done. I then colored the new outlines green, because I could.

You'll notice that because of how I dragged, the angles of the seams where the front and front-yoke will join have become more sloped automatically from the width change, which didn't change the armhole circumference, just as I wanted. I also wanted to add some shape to the back-to-yoke seam line, so I copied the new back outline to a new layer and dragged just the armhole of the

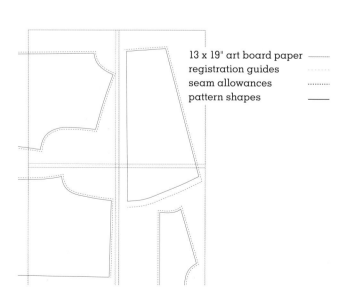

13 x 19" art board paper ———
registration guides - - - - - -
seam allowances ·············
pattern shapes ———

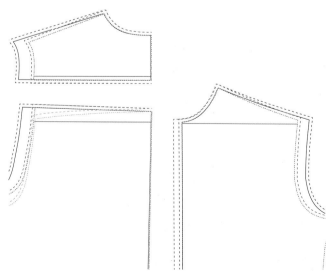

copy down (horizontally restrained) 1 inch (2.5 cm). I curved the now-angled back-to-yoke seam line slightly, then colored this new outline gold, unlocked the other layers, and added seam allowances all around.

I printed it and made a gingham muslin to see how it worked, shown above. Not perfect, but improved, I think, AND the pattern remains symmetrical, giving me a useful compromise when working with prominent plaids.

I could have done all this just as easily on paper with rulers and colored markers, and it might not have taken any more time. But the real key I think is the 11 x 17-inch (28 x 43 cm) scanner, which halves the effort of accurately digitizing patterns compared to smaller scanners and makes the whole enterprise suddenly feel reasonably efficient. You'll find further tutorials on using Illustrator for pattern work on my blog and listed in Resources.

You can do wonders with digital photography, too; there's even a "scanner" in my iPad that corrects distortions automatically if I shoot something rectangular but not square-on. The downside for subsequent pattern work is that any not-scanned images will have to be scaled to 1:1 by eye before you can print accurately—doable, but fiddly, potentially inaccurate, and time-consuming. But here are a few other interesting things I've found to do with digital photos and an image editor such as Photoshop. At bottom and right are two images both before and after tweaking in Photoshop to correct, in the first case, for perspective tilt (I used the gridded background as my guide), and in the second case, to make up for rulers not placed ideally in the original setup, a too-dark

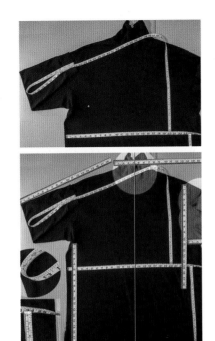

garment, a hard to read tape measure, and an unmarked center. There are many more tricks worth discovering once we digitize our sewing. I'll just leave you to mull over the image below, created in Illustrator; it shows the corrected front just demonstrated laid in red on top of the top-left scanned draft previously shown on page 20, which has been proportionately scaled up until its chest measure matches the red one's—no drafting required.

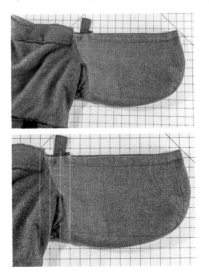

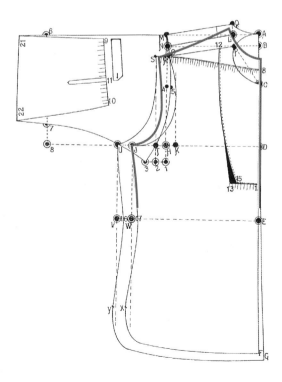

1

My Top 5 Design Lessons from Diane

1 The garment or pattern outline as a view-finder.
2 The garment or pattern piece as a cookie cutter.
3 The garment or pattern piece as a jigsaw puzzle.
4 The pattern outline as a phantom shape.
5 The seam line as a phantom link.

"Everything you bring to a project has equal value, but nothing leads: The pattern, your ideas, all your materials, your stash, all your experience, your skills, any of these can change your direction. Step aside from what you know and be ready to act on any idea."

2

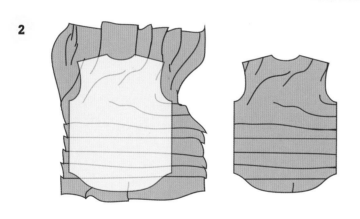

3

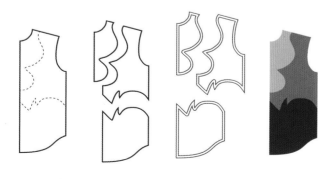

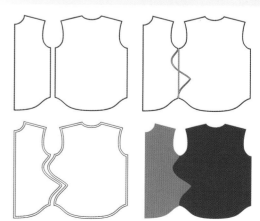

Diane Ericson

Nobody has turned on more light bulbs for me about playing with pattern shapes than my friend and unfailing inspirer of fresh ideas, Diane Ericson. Diane is the only person I've ever had the pleasure of hanging out with who truly improvises her way through every garment project. She and her legendary collaborator and mother, Lois, developed an amazing tool kit of finishing innovations and construction strategies that enable them and their horde of fervent students, readers, and pattern collectors to start sewing without knowing where they'll wind up, and to change direction effortlessly whenever inspiration calls for something better. At least a few of these depend so interestingly on my old workhorse, the core versus details, or block concept, that it was obvious I had to wind up my distinctly earthbound treatise on the topic with a glimpse of Diane's wild-blue-yonder virtuosity. A second or third look at many of her startling creations often reveals the solid foundation of really basic shapes, many of which are pure shirt. Diane is actually deeply fond of shirts, and delights in concocting new garments from cast-off, cut-up, deconstructed, rotated, inverted, painted, and drawn-upon ones. As she's told me many times, "I'm just looking for adventures I haven't had yet." And she's still managing to do them right inside her sewing studio.

4

5

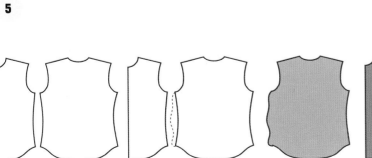

See the online resources for this book, my blog, and my Pinterest boards (ShirtmakingwithDPC) for working, and many more, links.

Buy a Better Pattern

Silhouettepatterns.com | This company is rare, if not unique, among pattern lines in offering all their women's top patterns with different fronts for different bust sizes. It works quite well, I'm told, and they offer many classic and contemporary shirts, blouses, and jackets with good shapes and simple directions. Lots of block sources here, plus many very interesting free video tutorials on fitting and factory construction.

Sewing.patternreview.com | A vast archive of patterns reviewed by members of this venerable community.

Take a Class/Buy a Custom Pattern

Sarahveblen.com | Sarah Veblen is the author of the current best-selling book on fitting and she's available for very reasonable one-on-one consultations, as of this writing, via email or Skype.

Deofsf.com | Don McCunn, author of one of my all-time favorite fitting books has retired from online classes but his mailing list is still quite active as of this writing, and he's putting all of his extensive class archives and videos online, including directions for making a custom form from the fitting body shell described in this book.

Paccprofessionals.org | The Association of Sewing and Design Professionals offers local and online referrals to sewing professionals in all areas of expertise, including fitting help and custom pattern making.

Drafting and Flat Pattern, Vintage

Shirts & Men's Haberdashery: 1840s to 1920s, by R. L. Shep and Gail Cariou. The best, if not only, all-in-one-place collection of old shirt drafting methods and books republished as facsimiles. Fascinating, but I wish it covered the 1900s more thoroughly. A good one to check out via interlibrary loan.

Drafting Men's Shirts and Undergarments, by Harry Simons. One of the best, most modern, and most varied draft books in the Cariou/Shep book above. It is also available at centerforpatternde-sign.com as a reprint, along with other cool related stuff.

Cutterandtailor.com | Has many large scans of more recent but still vintage drafts for shirts and much else, also linked to from my blog and boards.

Theperfectnose.wordpress.com | Has links to pdf downloads of many wonderful out-of-print drafting, draping, and design books from the 1930s and 1940s.

Drafting and Flat Pattern, Contemporary

The following three textbooks are college level, aimed at training garment industry pros, and are generally big and expensive, but they are comprehensive and filled with drafts for shirts (among other things), grading information, and industry terms and practices. They're all useful for home sewers, and each has many unique offerings. Find detailed, illustrated reviews of each on my blog.

Metric Pattern Cutting for Menswear, by Winifred Aldrich. Of the three, this is my favorite, but not by much. I like her many shirt and jacket blocks and directions, plus it's smaller than the others, and easier to hold!

The Practical Guide to Patternmaking for Fashion Designers—Menswear, by Lori A. Knowles.

Patternmaking for Menswear, by Gareth Kershaw.

Yourwardrobeunlockd.com | A wonderful, detailed blog post from a writer whose mother was an UrbanLegend designer, about how to draft like it was simple. Look under Articles/Free/Advanced for Pattern Drafting 1: Bodice Sloper.

Patternmaking Software

Cochenille.com | (garment designer, Mac and PC) and **wildginger.com** (pattern master, PC and via Windows emulation on the Mac). Both these companies have stuck it out through the boom and bust days of pattern making software for home sewers and continue to flourish because they love it and really understand

it. Especially useful if you sew for others, or ever make anything custom-fitted besides shirts.

Online Drafts

Googling "drafting men's shirt block," no quotes, will open the door to many resources, including these:

Lekala.co (yes, leave off the "m") | Lets you can order a free drafted shirt pattern for printing out at home after logging in and posting a few measurements, as well as many for-pay (but very inexpensive, and generally well reviewed) drafts for other styles for men, women, and children.

Damorrish.com/cadcam-downloads/menswear-shirt-block-generator | Offers other drafts besides shirts and lots of really useful tutorials on digital pattern work, for free.

Ralphpink.com/pattern-cutting/menswear/mens-basic-blocks | Offers other drafts besides shirts and lots of really useful tutorials on digital pattern work, for free.

Draping

Dress Design: *Draping and Flat Pattern Making*, by M. S. Hillhouse and Evelyn A. Mansfield. A timeless 1948 classic, in libraries everywhere and may even be still available in pdf form online for free.

Custom Forms

Sue-mason.com | Sue Mason has put together an amazing resource documenting her custom-molded body form discoveries in great detail, free, under Tutorials at her site. Thanks, Sue!

Visit my Pinterest boards for lots of links to other approaches, including the method I used for my form pictured through-out this book.

Copying

Kennethdking.com/book | *Making Garments from Existing Garments*, by Kenneth D. King. This excellent book on CD is very detailed and goes way beyond simply pin-copying dartless shirts. Kenneth offers many other methods on all aspects of pattern design, couture construction, and fitting.

Patternmaking for a Perfect Fit, by Steffani Lincecum . Another detailed approach to copying all sorts of garments and making patterns from them. Steffani also offers an online class on the topic at craftsy.com.

Tools

NONDIGITAL

Amazon.com is the current source for my favorite new curved rulers and rolling measuring devices, **SA rulers**; really cool and useful! Check out my Pinterest boards for links to all the other tools described in this chapter.

DIGITAL

Epson WorkForce WF-7510 | This is my super-scanner/printer for 11 x 17-inch (28 x 43 cm) tabloid-size paper, aka Ledger or B size, and Super- B, or 13 x1 9-inch (33 x 48 cm), print only. If you're beginning to really enjoy downloadable patterns, this is your secret weapon.

To Consider

Considering that the presumed goal of all pattern-drafting instruction is to get students to eventually no longer need any patterns or directions to come up with a new pattern for what they want to design, I suggest—if this is even a little bit your goal, too—spending some time with scaled-down diagrams of garment pattern pieces such as you'll find in pattern-piece thumbnails (vintage patterns sales at Etsy and eBay often include them), books on design, and some costume-history texts (the Dover book shown here is excellent). At first, just imagine how you'd draw up a full-size pattern from only these little diagrams, with a fitting block as the foundation, and then actually try it! Maybe start with just a detail, like the collars here, and think of it as a drawing exercise. How much more information do you really need to begin playing?

CHAPTER 2

Skills and Structures

When I started sewing as an adult I had the idea that I needed to find the "best" techniques for whatever I wanted to sew. Gradually I began to see that while different methods did usually mean different results or different features for any given process, any method for sewing anything could be done well; it was the skill more than the steps that made the difference. So I switched to looking for the methods that would get the best results without practice, which some methods seem to require a great deal of! I simply didn't—and don't—have the time to develop a lot of skills, especially compared to factory sewers who do the same thing many hundreds of times every day. But as an art major in college, I did start out with something I think is equally valuable: an appreciation of craftsmanship.

I was sloppy at crafts as a kid, and couldn't understand how my better-at-it peers often did such amazing stuff. Were my hands faulty? In college I finally got that the way forward in any craft is, first, to simply be willing to take the time to do something well, to do whatever it will take to realize a goal. After all, very little good art is accomplished by putting in the least necessary effort. And often the easiest thing to be struck by with anything well made is how much time it must have taken, either in preparatory training or in execution, and usually both.

So, I came to sewing realizing that if I were willing to take the care and time with it that I'd learned to apply to a drawing or painting, I could eventually get my projects to turn out pretty well. In other words, even though the specific skills needed would be brand new, the basic craftsmanship required was the same and certainly transferable. So, even if I wasn't willing or able to put in lots of practice time, I WAS willing to go as slow and as carefully as I needed to in order to get good results.

Craftsmanship applies with equal force no matter the finish level of the project you're working on. A T-shirt or a jeans jacket requires a different level of finish and ingredients—and different skills—than, say, a wedding gown or a tailored suit coat, but the degree to which craftsmanship will ensure good results is about the same, I find.

Exactly what good results are is subject to quite a lot of variation, of course, and can very reasonably be revised on a per-project or even per-detail basis, and downward revisions are just as plausible as upward ones depending on the project. Being vague about the standards, though, is a recipe for trouble, since you'll naturally be inclined to be satisfied with whatever you come up with first try! I still get my own standards mostly from manufactured clothes, but also frequently from custom-made and hand-crafted things. Expanding my standards one of my chief pleasures and goals as I

cruise the Internet these days, and one of the most active areas of innovation amongst designers at every level of our craft. Alabama Chanin's wonderfully hand-stitched knit garments are a current case in point.

The garments I'm considering in this "shirt" book can potentially cover a really wide range of finish levels, and the pattern shapes I'm offering can all be deployed at any level of finish you require. After all these years, it's still clear that no matter what method I'm trying out or at what finish level I'm working, I'll need to:

1 Be certain up front what the steps will be.

2 Have a clear standard in mind for the quality I want to achieve.

3 Cut out and stitch accurately. Go as slow as needed.

4 Press at every stage, with great attention to the shapes I want the iron to create or establish.

And most important:

5 ALWAYS make a sample. Test everything.

It works . . . for me.

I'm definitely still collecting methods and tools that reduce practice time and improve my efficiency. In this chapter I'll share the main ones I find pertinent for shirtmaking. Be assured that if you like some other methods better I won't argue!

What I'm calling "structures" here are ways of arranging, folding, or manipulating fabric layers for common details that also apply regardless of finish level, for the most part. My approach to them comes from my first requirement in the list above: understanding what I'm doing. I had lots of experiences when I started sewing of going through a sequence of steps with no real idea of what exactly I'd done when it was over, even if it turned out okay. Slowing down to "get" the structure behind the steps has always led to better results, and more interestingly, to more flexibility when coming up with either new, related details or new ways to assemble the thing to begin with. My intention here is to dissect a few of these quickly and graphically so the structures feel easily graspable, and are also seen as generic, not specific to any particular project or pattern shapes, but extendable and morphable as needed. Fingers crossed this works for you! The detailed, specific treatments are mostly to be found in the online content, where the space for going into a lot of detail is not constrained.

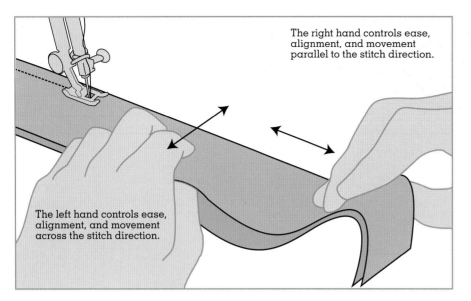

The right hand controls ease, alignment, and movement parallel to the stitch direction.

The left hand controls ease, alignment, and movement across the stitch direction.

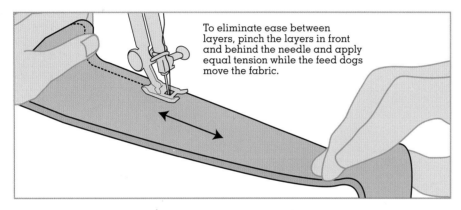

To eliminate ease between layers, pinch the layers in front and behind the needle and apply equal tension while the feed dogs move the fabric.

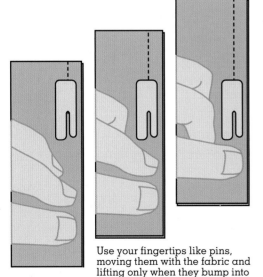

Use your fingertips like pins, moving them with the fabric and lifting only when they bump into the foot.

To add ease, stitch a single layer while holding it back right behind the needle, pausing to let go every few inches to let it relax.

Sewing without Pins

I read a book with this title early on in my sewing days and it made a big difference in my results. It was the first time I'd thought about anything as basic as how to hold the fabric when machine stitching, let alone whether or not to use pins. I found the information about controlling ease by how you hold the fabric a lot more useful than the often encountered idea that you were to simply "let the feed dogs do it" by putting a longer layer on the bottom next to them.

There's no reason to revise or abandon any other method of sewing you're already happy with. Still, these ideas are in wide use among professional machine operators and, you'll notice them often, especially in online sewing demos, and I encourage you to try them out.

I'm especially impressed with the method at left for adding ease or even light gathers, even though applying it precisely does take some testing. But it's easy to adjust the results you get and faster to apply than stitching over gathering threads. It's ideal for gathering a back into a yoke edge. Marcy Tilton uses it to reduce rippling when topstitching knit hems with a double needle, so it's not just applicable to single layers. I also often find it faster and more accurate to join opposing curves as I sew than to pin them together beforehand, particularly with collars and sleeves sewn flat.

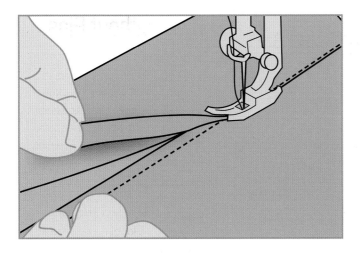

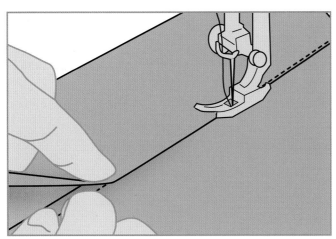

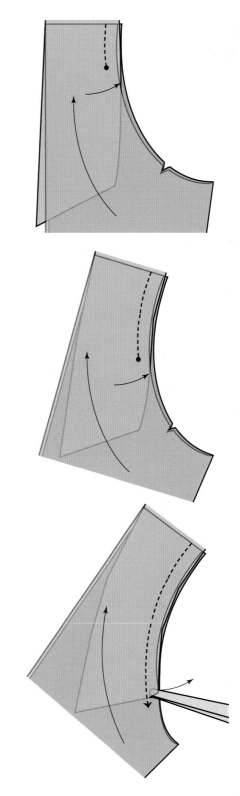

When edgestitching to match and cover a previous seam, as on a collar stand or cuff, form the edge as it's being stitched, stopping with the needle down and lifting the top layer frequently to confirm alignment, then "pinning" precisely with a fingertip.

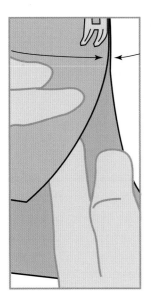

Align curved edges only as they're about to go under the foot, swinging the edges together gradually as they move forward together. Park the needle down anytime you need a shift you can't make in motion, aiming to arrange only the inch (2.5 cm) or so that's about to go under the foot.

When joining a collar to a faced, curved neckline, pivot the body/facing unit to keep it aligned with the foot as you swing the collar edges in between toward the neckline edges. Blunt-tipped tweezers can be very helpful when you reach a corner or tip in a tight spot.

Stitching Seams

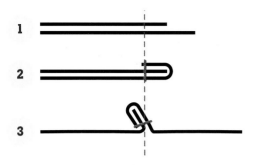

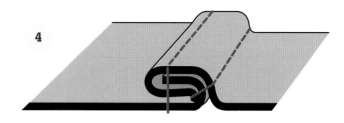

Machine-Turned Felling

If using a felling presser foot to form the seam, (1) start with right sides together with the seam allowances cut unevenly, one to match the foot's width, placed on top, and the other twice that. (2) The first pass through the foot wraps the wider allowance over the narrower and secures all layers. (3) Press the seam open from the right side, then press the allowances over the seam line. (4) The second pass closes the seam the foot's width away.

Only the second-pass stitches are visible on the right side, but you can reverse the layers if you want two rows of stitching on the outside, perhaps to simulate the look of industrial double stitching,

shown at right. This method is sometimes referred to as "Single-Needle Tailoring" precisely to distinguish it from double-needle work, typically associated with heavy-duty construction, sportswear, and work wear.

Presser feet for wide (8 mm) and narrow (4 mm) felled seams are available for all machines, but the wider ones can distort the wider allowances they require, especially on thin fabrics, which are easy enough to handle by hand as described next. The narrower seams are quite challenging to manage neatly without the help of a foot, in my experience.

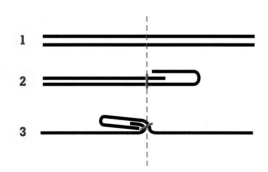

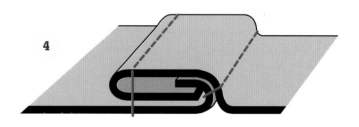

Hand-Turned Felling

If not using a felling foot, the seam allowances are often not trimmed before stitching, and the finished seam width is dependent on the width of the original seam allowances. Various sequences are possible, the one shown being typical: (1) Stitch the seam right sides together with your preferred seam allowance. (2) Trim the upper allowance close to the stitching, at least slightly less than half the starting width, then press the wider lower layer over it, aligning the raw edge with the seam line. (3) Press the seam open from the right side, then press both allowances over

the seam line. (4) Close the seam by stitching parallel to both the original seam line and the pressed-under edge.

It makes no difference to the strength of the seam if the folded-under layer wraps around the trimmed layer, or sits on top of it, so if you'd prefer to press the seam open in step 1 before trimming, and then press the folded allowance over the trimmed one, that will work equally well.

Faux Felling (Serged Welt)

If the raw edges of the seam allowances will be serged together—either after forming the seam or at the same time—or in some other way finished (perhaps with an overlocking stitch from a zigzag-capable machine), there's no need to fold them under or to trim the hidden edge before stitching through all layers parallel to the original seam.

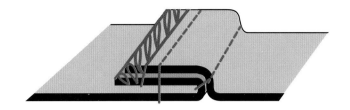

Double Stitched (Industrial Only)

A very common finish on manufactured shirts, this is created with a specialized and dedicated device called a Double Needle Feed-Off-the-Arm Chain Stitch Sewing Machine. The machine wraps the layers together and stitches them twice (or with three rows, if preferred), all in a single pass. Note that both seam lines in this case are chain-stitched (the "chain" is on the wrong side), not lock-stitched as in all the above, and both lines are visible on either side.

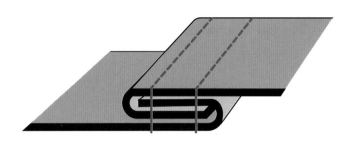

Non-Programmed Keyholes and Buttonholes 📖

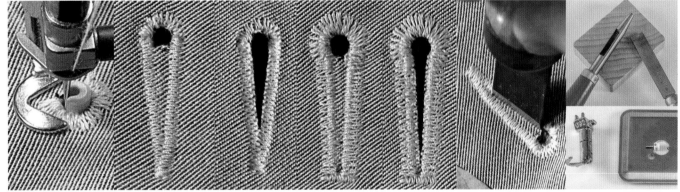

With an eyelet presser-foot plate and a zigzag machine, you can make higher quality keyhole and other buttonhole shapes than you can with most preprogrammed simulations, as shown above, complete with stitches that wrap around a precut opening at one end; more detailed directions are online. Even without an eyelet plate, you can get great results just by stitching satin stitches in an elongated, diamond shape, as shown at left, and cutting out later with a chisel and an eyelet cutter.

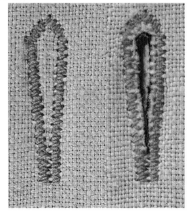

Turn a Better Point

Most home-sewing methods involve a stitching adjustment at the point, along with close trimming of the allowances (A) before pushing out a turned point. Diagrams 1-4 show the approach I've seen in use by professionals, which is different in every respect, except for the idea of keeping the interfacing out of the point area, which is generally a good idea but not essential. The pro method is to stitch straight all the way to the point, either pivoting or crossing as shown (1), and then to fold the allowances over the point without trimming them (2, 3), thereby creating from the start the flattest and most pointed arrangement possible. The hard part is

to maintain this arrangement while turning, which they do by folding over the tip again and pinching it while turning as shown at left, step 4, with one finger up inside the unturned collar. The logic of all this is great, but that last step definitely requires practice. So I add an aid in the form of some strong but narrow tweezers tips, which lets me hold the folds right at the actual point and skip the extra folding over. There's usually still some unturned material, and a heavy needle in the seam works great to level that out while also flattening any bumping outward at the side (B). You can get the best of both methods by trimming only one layer at the tip, leaving the other for folding (C). When folding right-angled corners and greater, you can skip folding the tip down first.

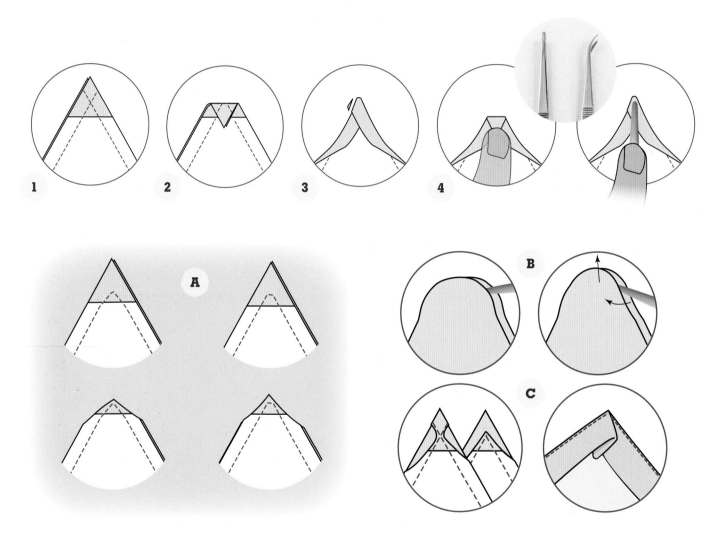

Use Templates for Repeating Precision

Any edge I need to fold and press under exactly or symmetrically, I always turn over an oak tag or manila template, which itself needs to be precisely shaped of course, with careful drawing and cutting. This is definitely worth doing even if you think you'll never use the same shape again. Take the time once and enjoy the elegant results every time you wear the garment. Some light glue stick dabs will hold the pressed-under seam allowances when pressing the whole thing from the right side, and a little spray sizing or starch is often helpful to stabilize the final pressed shape during subsequent construction or topstitching. Use the glue stick to hold details like pockets in place while topstitching, too.

The Burrito Method

So dubbed because it involves wrapping all or part of your work into a tight roll inside the layers you need to stitch, this method often allows you to trim corners more easily and extensively than other methods, as shown in the cuff example at bottom. It's also a neat way to attach a yoke without any visible stitches, turning out the rolled layers at one end or through the neck. If I'm going to edgestitch the yoke anyway, I don't bother doing this, because it's not so easy to keep the yoke layers equal and it wrinkles the rolled-up layers. I love it for collars and cuffs, as described in detail in my first book and online.

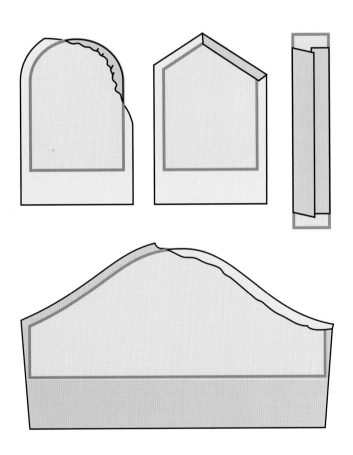

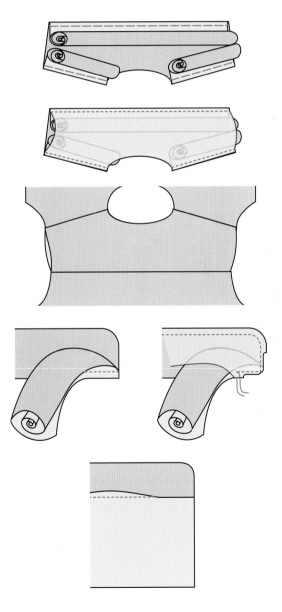

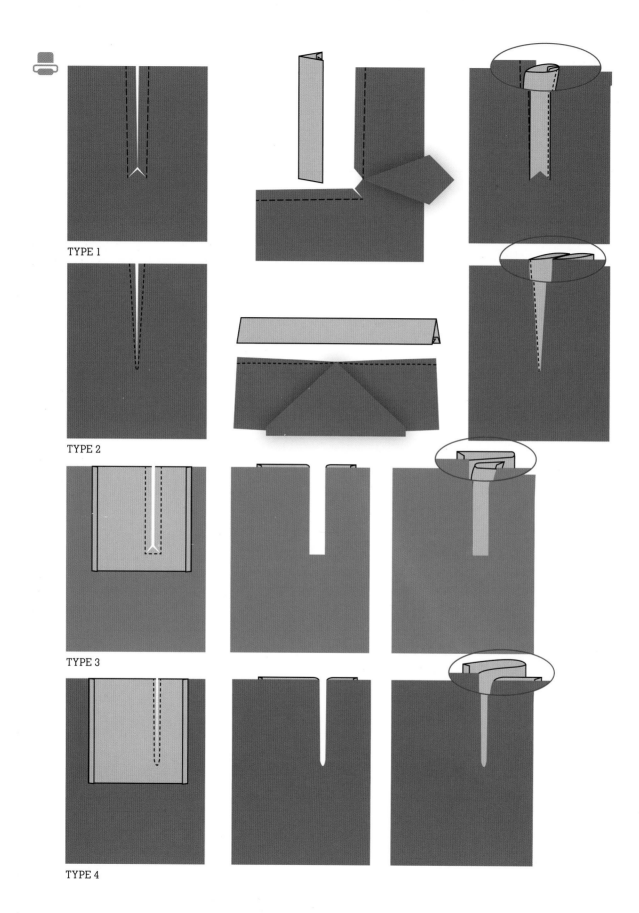

TYPE 1

TYPE 2

TYPE 3

TYPE 4

Placket Origami

A placket is any structure designed to create an overlap and an underlap at a slash or cut in an unseamed area of a garment, such as above the ends of a cuff on a sleeve or at the neckline of a pull-over shirt. There are many ways to build one, but they seem to boil down to at least four main types, as shown at left, all of which can be varied either subtly or radically, as demonstrated with the few examples here. For all four placket types, the slash line is marked first, then reinforced with stitches on either side of the mark before cutting. These stitches are parallel; spaced equally far apart at the start and end of the slash (1 and 3); or tapering, starting farther from the slash at the open end and tapering or curving to a point just below the end of the slash (2 and 4), which offers the option of concealing the placket entirely inside the garment. The slashes on 1 and 2 are reinforced and cut before adding the placket fabric; the slashes on 3 and 4 are reinforced with the stitches that add the placket material, then cut through all layers.

Type 1 is very flexible and workable to any desired width on either placket piece. It's easy to match the widths of the two lapping layers and fabric pattern matching is easy. Some topstitching and the buttonholes could be done before joining the placket, especially on wider plackets. See the Folk Block chapter for variations on this type.

Type 2 is the familiar "continuous bound strip" found everywhere. It's fast, flexible, and soft, and requires no additional finishing once the binding is secured on both sides of the slash, unlike any other type. There's no right or wrong side if you don't further stitch it

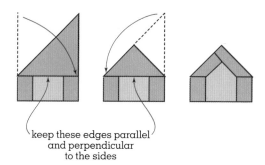

keep these edges parallel
and perpendicular
to the sides

down in some way, so it's pretty much the only one suitable for reversible garments, and it's by far the fastest, start to finish, of all types to make. There's no easy way to vary the lap widths or match patterns. There's a common, if bulky, variation at top left below, which creates a right-triangular tip automatically, but it's eight layers thick, not counting allowances.

Type 3 is the one I described in *Shirtmaking* and generally prefer. It's the most common type found on high-end shirts assembled as shown below at left. It's easy to vary dramatically (examples on the next page) and easy to apply because it can be completely formed by pressing and thus checked before stitching. Pattern matching is easy, but it's not easy to make the laps equal width.

Type 4 is the one typically found on polo shirt center-front openings. It offers much more flexibility than type 2 in the design of the binding shape's outer edges (good for facings, etc.). Either side could be planned and shaped to be the right side. It requires careful pattern making as well as skillful sewing and slashing.

I find glue sticks invaluable for many processes, especially when making type-3 plackets. First, toss it if it's dried out and rubbery like the upper example below right; it should be like butter. I use a pin tip to apply it precisely in small places, such as under the folds at the triangle tip, to keep the folds down and when positioning the point on the sleeve's right side and matching a pattern before stitching it down.

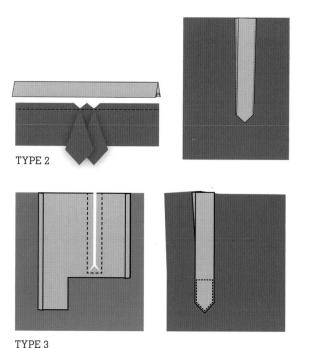

TYPE 2

TYPE 3

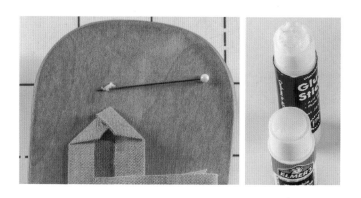

Type 3 Placket Variations

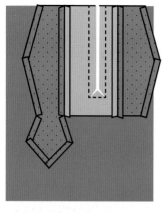   

The potential for placket variation is effectively infinite. The simplest thing is just to change the dimensions and/or the proportions of the layers. Any placket edge that's the last one on either side to be topstitched down could also be converted from a straight fold to some other shape and be extended beyond the usual edge. The extension could then be shaped in any way you like for more topstitching or edge finishing. Further, any free folded edge on a finished placket could be changed from a fold to a seam, allowing for bulk reduction (the hidden layers could be a lighter weight fabric) and freeing all edges of the outer, visible layer from any need to remain straight, all as shown in the type-3 examples. And as you can see below, this same structure can be as easily converted to a pocket opening just by slashing in the middle of the fabric instead of the edge and stitching around both ends. In fact, if started from the garment right side, type 3 with slightly different origami is also one typical structure used for welted pockets. My favorite adaptation of type 3 is the cowboy-shirt cuff, such as the one at left, which expands on the example above by adding piping and extending into a facing around the entire sleeve hem. All the other types could also be adapted to pockets or mid-garment openings, but only types 1 and 3 are easily suited to the job.

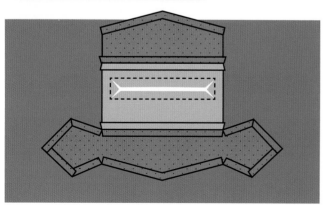 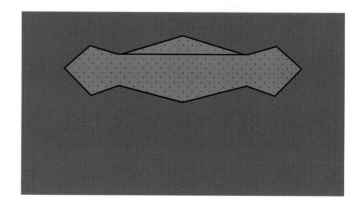

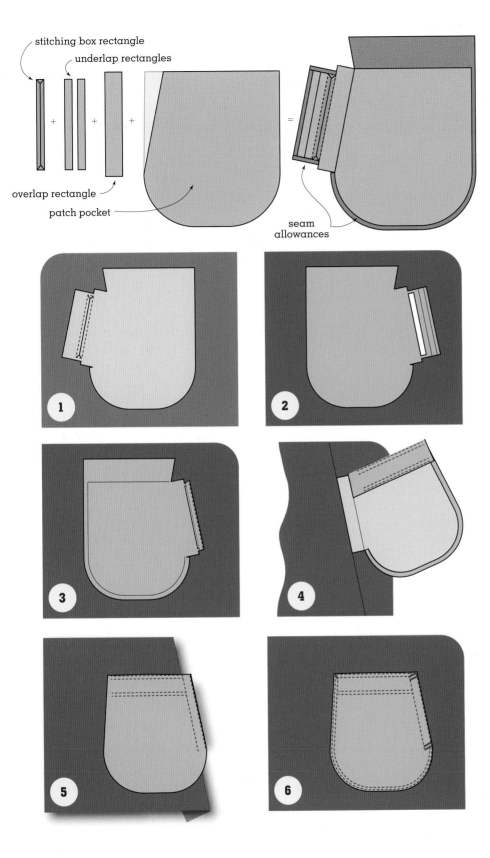

stitching box rectangle

underlap rectangles

overlap rectangle

patch pocket

seam allowances

Without a pocket bag layer underneath, a placket finished on all sides becomes an opening with over- and underlapping edges, ideal for through-the-shirt access to pants pockets on a long shirt-jacket. Add a pocket bag layer on the wrong side between the placket piece(s) and the garment layers, turn the placket through them both, and you'll have a pocket, anywhere and at any angle you want.

Here's another option: Extend the placket into a patch pocket, AND include a through-garment opening at the edge.

Build the pattern from the starting shape of the reinforcing stitches' rectangle (at least 5 1/2 inches [14 cm] long, to allow the hand to go through), plus two underlap rectangles that match the stitched one, plus one overlap rectangle wider (I doubled it) and longer (by about 1/2 inch [1.3 cm] on each end) than the stitched box. Join all these to a large shaped patch pocket, which will be the outer overlap layer, and then add seam allowances. Except for the few additional edges that need folding and stitching as the patch pocket is formed, the basic sequence is exactly the same as for a standard type-3 placket. This pattern and step-by-step directions are online as usual.

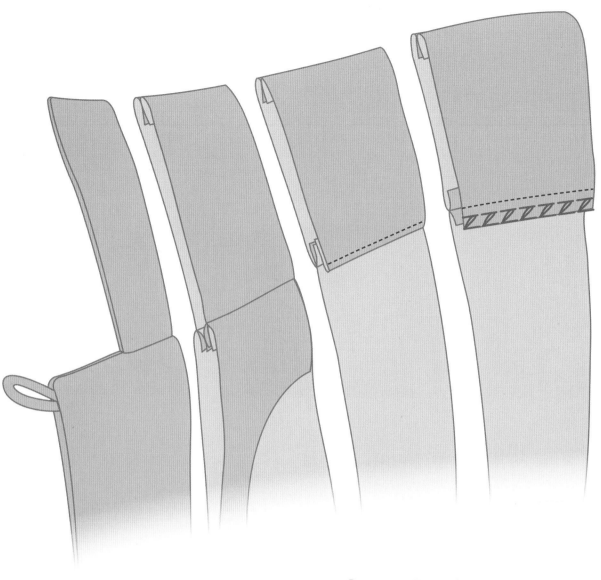

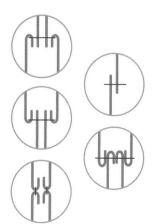

Convertible Collar Options

Conventional wisdom has it that there are three options for the seam allowances at the neckline of any garment with a collar: up into the collar or stand, down into the garment, or pressed open, as in the little diagrams at far left. There's actually two others in common use, near left, one of which is a simple overlap of finished edges and the other a simple overlap of turned-under edges. And the whole story is really that most shirt collars exhibit a mix of approaches within a single collar, differing both between ends and middle, and inner and outer. All the common treatments are diagrammed in the cutaways above, and the variations are so profuse that I've assembled the most useful into separate printable direction sheets, such as the one peeking out at us at right, and put them online.

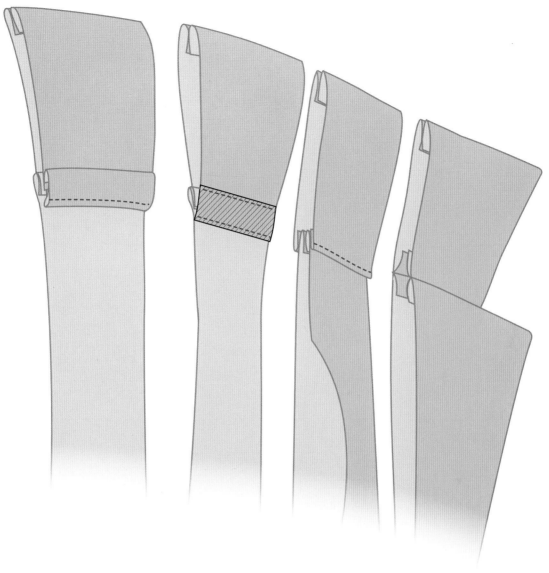

Convertible Collar Construction; no back facing

Variation 2: Overcast or Bound Seam Allowances at Back Neckline

 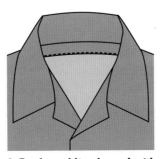 

| Options: | 1. Back neckline overcast | 2. Back neckline bound with bias self- or lining fabric | 3. Back neckline bound with tape |

Size 36
Size 40
Size 38
Size 38
Size 38
Size 38
Size 38
Size 36
Size 36
Size 36
Size 36

JEDEDIAH PANTS
Back Yoke
Cut 2 Self

JEDEDIAH PANTS
Back
Cut 2 Self

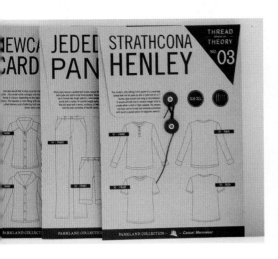

Morgan Meredith

Sewist Blogging Compleat

Thread Theory, the creation of Morgan Meredith and her husband Matt, is a pattern line for menswear (and for women who like to wear it) with a very welcome emphasis on knits. To my eye, their site perfectly exemplifies everything that contemporary sewing and blogging offers the rest us fortunate home sewers: unique and versatile patterns, savvy tutorials and links, detailed sew-alongs, and pertinent, inviting glimpses inside the life of other dedicated sewing maniacs as they innovate, exhilarate . . . and collapse, just like we do, or hope to do. As soon as I found it, I knew I'd enjoy connecting with them, and sharing their wisdom and experiences. As tireless and generous with her correspondence as apparently with all else she does, Morgan sent me a huge trove of information about her design process; here it is.

Styling Menswear (Using Line, Color, and Texture)

I think that it is uncommon to find stylish and current menswear sewing patterns because of the common misconception that menswear is too boring to waste valuable sewing time on. I firmly believe that menswear is just as interesting if not more interesting than dresses and skirts as a sewing project. Sewers designing and constructing menswear projects are more confined to convention than if they were to sew a women's garment if they are hoping to create something that is easily (and willingly!) worn in public. While some may see this as a limitation of sewing menswear, I see it as an advantage because working within convention more thoroughly emphasizes challenging aspects, such as sewing precision, knowledge of fabric properties, and creativity, when faced with creating an original garment while meeting established criteria.

When sewing menswear, it is very important to remember the three elements of garment design: line, color, and texture. These three elements operate as percentages that must always result in a full 100 percent. For instance, if a sewer decides to emphasize color by choosing a neon green fabric, it is important to choose a fabric that does not also highlight an unusual texture as well as a common pattern that results in a common silhouette. Of course, these three elements are just guidelines to help create a conventional and wearable menswear garment, and they can easily be broken if the goal is to create something exciting, shocking, and fashion-forward! To explain how these concepts can be used to create a modern and fashionable menswear garment, here is how I approach sewing a Newcastle Cardigan:

Line: Line is the silhouette and fit of a garment. When using a sewing pattern, such as our Newcastle Cardigan pattern, a lot of the choices when designing the line of a garment have already been made for the sewer by the pattern designer. By choosing to sew the Newcastle Cardigan, I have decided I want to create a slim-fitting knit garment suited to a fairly slim and tall wearer. I have decided the garment's focus will be the cozy shawl collar and that the cardigan will have youthful, extra-long sleeves and a short body reminiscent of a motorcycle jacket. Of course, if any one of these features doesn't fit the line that I, as the sewer, want to achieve, the pattern can be altered to achieve a different fashion fit (more on this later!).

To read more, see the complete article online.

Embrace Twill Tape

If you've examined any new casual shirts lately, especially knit ones, you're likely to have encountered treatments like those above, in which twill tape is used to reinforce and bind, even create entire plackets. Any truly woven, selvedge-edged tape or ribbon will serve, as will bias binding, but with more effort—and there are plenty of options. The source with the most real variety that I've found is etsy.com.

Pressing Gear, Bought and Made

Here are the pressing tools that I rely upon every day sitting upon the most useful one of all: a homemade pressing board (plywood, woolen layers, wrapped in heavy linen) that sits where needed as needed. It is as useful as a pinnable surface as a pressing one (see it at work when scanning garments in the Dress Block chapter). Don't make it too big to toss around, or too small for a couple of collar pieces: mine is 16 x 24 inches (40.5 x 61 cm). A clapper is more than a pressing tool; it's also a much-used pressing surface. Nothing is better for a hard crease, as at the end of a placket, so bigger is better. With the sleeve board and point presser nearby, I almost never open my regular ironing board, or expose the pressing surface (made the same) that covers my entire cutting table, under the cutting mat. A cotton twill and a Teflon press cloth complete the kit. I don't like the holes in steam irons and don't miss having one, and sometimes a little stiffing from starch or sizing is just what's needed to make a sewing process become easy.

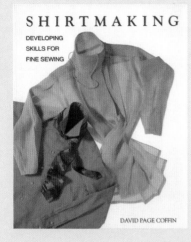 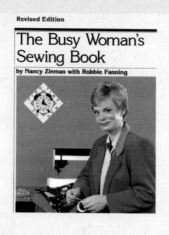 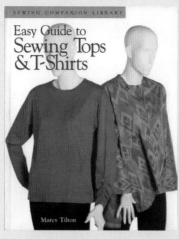 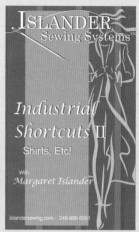

My first sewing book, *Shirtmaking*, is everything I figured out about dress-shirt making over ten years of testing and research, disguised at the last minute into looking like a general shirtmaking book. It's not; this one is more like that.

There's plenty of unique shirt-making skills and tips in both these books, by Marcy Tilton and Nancy Zeiman—two Giants among the Sewing Giants of my boomer era. Don't miss!

Neither should any shirtmaker miss Margaret Islander's classic video workshop on pinless, industrial sewing techniques applied to classic sport-shirt making. It's definitely an essential, and many say, a life-changing experience.

Master shirtmaker Anna Gorbatenko is the featured designer in the dress-shirt chapter. I once asked her to outline her collar-making process for me via email, because it's a variation of my technique, but with heavy fusibles instead of medium-weight sew-ins as I'm used to and describe in my other book. She astounded me with a gloriously put-together sew-along with more than seventy huge, clear photos of her entire process—from drafting to the final hand stitches—that are her trademark. The whole thing is now in your hands, via this book's online content. Thank you, Anna!

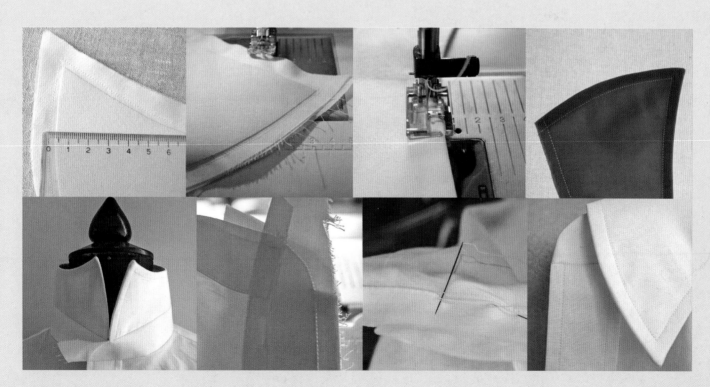

CHAPTER 3

The Dress (or Shaped) Shirt Block

I 'll start each block chapter by presenting and dissecting a range of featured garments, both in the book and online as space permits, that seem to me to exemplify some important features of the category; I'll sometimes also show how the category might be stretched. Larger pictures, and more of them, will be online for each garment featured in the print pages. Then I'll discuss the details and unique techniques that I find most interesting, present the patterns and/or process steps I've collected, and sometimes wind up with a featured artist or expert and pertinent reference resources, as described in the introduction. Complete patterns for the featured garments aren't provided, except in cases where I'm the designer, but in other cases a detail or two inspired by each garment is available, ready to pop onto your own blocks as you like, for best-fitting results.

The Dress Shirt

Garments of this type commonly include shirts suitable for wearing with a tie, evening and formal shirts, close-fitting uniform shirts, sporty shirts with the same sort of collars and fit, Western shirts (because these are rarely loose), equestrian shirts, and the like. What I'm calling a dress shirt commonly has these features:

Fit

Bodies that are often shaped at the sides, underarms, and yoke so they fit the figure somewhat to quite closely, and can be comfortably worn under other not-too-loose garments, such as suit and sport jackets, close-fitting sweaters, vests, and larger shirt blocks.

If you have several shirt blocks, this would be the most closely fitting one, or the one with the least intentional added ease, especially at the shoulders and neck, where this block has little or no change from a fitted body shell. These are under- and single-layer garments for the most part.

Of course the degree of closeness or shaping wanted here will vary by individual, by age, by purpose, by group, as well as by fashion. My first shirt patterns were all from this category, but what I've wanted from a "dress" shirt body has varied dramatically over the years.

Details

A dress shirt has band collars, collars with separate stands, or collars cut to have a stand and a fall portion with a defined, static roll line; all are cut to fit a high, close neckline that buttons at the neck. Yokes are typical, more often high and small, than low and deep. It can have short or long sleeves, and if long, it has close-fitting cuffs and sleeves long enough so the cuffs will extend beyond those of the garments worn over them. Above the cuffs, deep placket openings allow for easy rolling up of the sleeves. Hems are usually shaped and finished with a simple roll or some other bulk-free edging, facilitating being unobtrusively tucked into and worn beneath the bottom garment.

Fabrics

The fabric is woven, more likely than not to be lightweight and crisp, certainly washable, but also medium-weight and soft; it is not very likely to be heavy, insulating, or stiff. These garments are generally not outerwear, although the details here can and have certainly been adapted to outerwear fabrics and blocks.

I'm not sure what vintage this attached-collar formal evening shirt is; I'll guess the 1950s.

Among the first things one notices with this shirt in person is the very gauzy, lightweight body fabric, typical of older formal shirts like the one shown front and back at top right, and chosen not as a seasonal feature but simply to keep the wearer as cool and bulk-free as possible under the vest and tux assumed to be worn over it at all times in public, concealing all but the bib, collar, and cuffs, which were all that needed to be crisp and opaque. Shirts, after all, were for many centuries considered underwear, the first layer protecting more important and substantial garments from the skin, and vice versa.

Bib fronts are a classic shirt detail with endless potential for design play well beyond the formal shirt. A century or more ago, they were part of most shirts, from dressy to outdoor, usually as an insert pieced into the body, as with both of the vintage garments shown here. Full advantage was taken of the opportunity the bib seams offer for more or less invisibly shaping the front by shaping the seams that join to the bib, as shown in the scans from old drafts at center right. A and B show a full chest adaptation, and at far right is a full waist trick.

These days, especially if the garment isn't intended as formal "underwear," pleated fronts are simply cut onto the shirt as extra width, and run all the way to the hem if intended to be worn untucked, or if wanted shorter, simply patched onto the full shirt front as an appliqué, as shown at lower right. Neither approach precludes the concealment of a vertical shoulder dart cut parallel to and just inside the outermost pleat or the side of the patch. A striped shirt body probably isn't the best choice in either case, unless you want to make a virtue of the obvious angles that will appear.

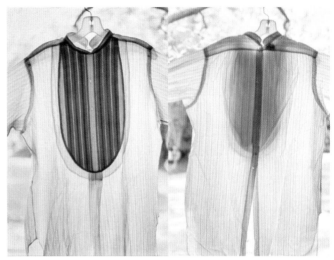

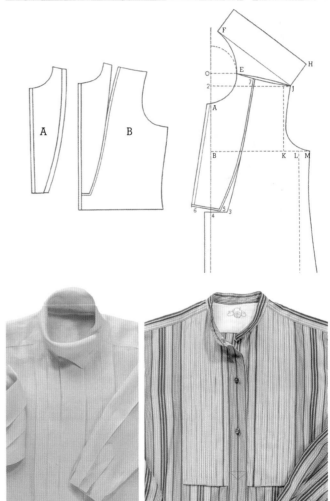

The bib on this shirt is inserted with a double-needle, chain-stitched, wrapped seam on the sides and a fold-over seam covered with a fabric strip at the bottom, as shown inside and out at far left. From one bib bottom all the way to the hem and around the back to the other side bib, the edges are finished with a narrow, machine-rolled hem (top near left), into which are placed small folded inserts, including the button/buttonhole facing strips at far left (I love how the ends of these are simply folded over at a right angle to catch in the rolled hem as well), and the side-seam gussets at center, near left, shown from both sides. (Directions for the single-needle version online.) Note how the double-needle chained side-seam stitching more or less blends into the hem roll, confirming that the hems were done first.

At bottom near left are the sleeve vent, with its lightweight continuous-strip placket, topstitched at the top of the opening through just the overlap side of the strip and the sleeve, and then the yoke, which reveals the double-needle finish at the armhole, just like the side and underarm seams. Note the subtle but persistent ease added on all three pieces that join to it: front, sleeve cap, and back.

Most interesting of all, I think, is the unusual collar, stand, and neckline shown at right; the top is from the outside and the next is from the inside. This is designed to bring the collar ends right to the neckline with no visible stand in front and thus no coverage of the neck itself there. The collar ends and tie will sit directly on the chest, not a common look these days, and one more easily achieved by simply dropping the neckline in front and adding enough cone-like up-curve (as described a few pages along) to the stand ends so they fall against the chest.

Nonetheless, I find it fascinating how the maker responded to this cut-off stand at the collar end by covering the neckline seam with a thin, self-fabric strip—as opposed to a facing, much the simpler and more expected treatment, I'd have thought—exactly as we'll see sometimes done with camp- and knit-collared shirts in the chapters to come. An impressive bit of stitchery bringing all those multilayered ends and edges together under such a tiny strip with such neatly folded-under allowances and precision edgestitching, mirroring the inside treatment at the bottom of the pleated bib.

Garments Profiled online:

Territory Ahead Silk Twill

Author-made Eastern/Western

Charvet Women's Dress

Featured Technique

Arranging and adjusting a paper strip directly on the body or form is my preferred way to customize the shape of bands and stands to a particular body; I regard it as draping. Working on top of a garment, as in the images at far right, seems like it would add the needed ease for a comfortable circumference, but it's easier and more flexible to adapt the length later from simple measurements of the particular necklines. The draping here is more about the shape of the band than the length of it, which can be easily adjusted as needed. For that purpose, I prefer to work without a garment underneath, and then to lay a neckline reference on top, as shown below, using either an already fitted muslin neckline template, as in the upper images, or another measured paper rectangle dropped on top, as in the lower images.

With the test strip directly on the form or body and no reference underneath, you're free to let the strip find its own best position, particularly in back. Dropping a muslin neckline over it when it looks good lets you confirm the neckline, and pin-poking through it transfers the line to the paper.

Another paper strip formed into a cylinder of the right neckline circumference works well, too, when dropped over a shaped band; although it's less stable, it can still provide a reference for marking a curve that appears straight from the side. Note that it was necessary to clip the stand paper in front to get it to lie flat for marking.

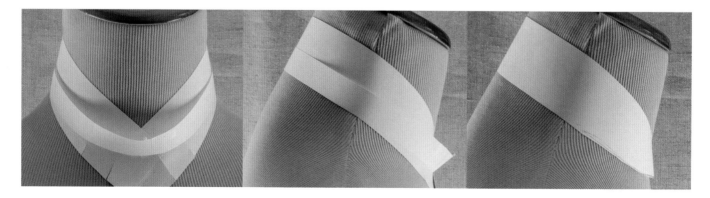

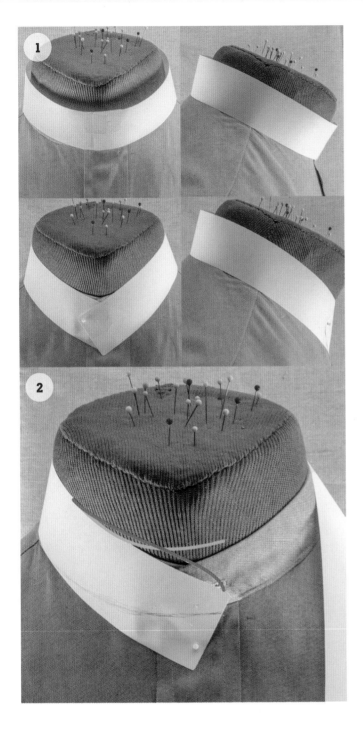

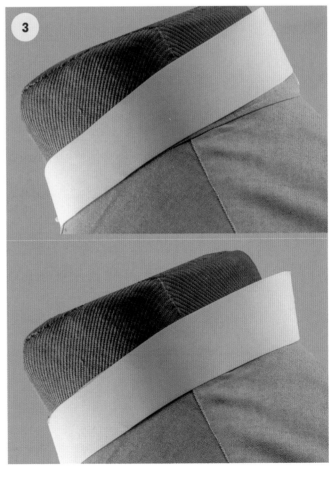

1. (Top, L and R) A rectangular paper strip wrapped squarely around the neck creates a cylinder shape that doesn't follow the neck contours. (Bottom, L and R) Allowing the front ends of the rectangle to dip and cross at an angle at the center-front tapers the front, and to a lesser extent the sides, of the cylinder into a cone shape that brings it closer to the neck. Note that the back remains untapered.

2. Tracing the neckline onto the lower front edges of the rectangle shows how to curve the front of the paper into the start of a band or stand pattern. When the original marked rectangle is traced, the upper edge can also be redrawn to curve in various similar ways.

3. Raising the back of the paper strip on this particular neck so it no longer dips in back, as does the garment underneath, brings the strip much closer to the neck and adds a little more room in front. The corresponding pattern change is to raise the back neckline so it and the lower edge of the attached bands and collars are as straight as possible, as seen from the side.

	1	**2**	**3**
Cylinder			
Cone			
Nested Cones			
Plate			

1 Between them, these geometric "primitives" pretty much cover the options for dress collars, necklines, stands, and bands. The top three are clearly collar and band shapes, but the plate is both the neckline and a collar type as well, because it could be regarded as an extreme type of flattened cone, and it could certainly be joined to itself along either edge. The main thing these all have in common is that they'd all sit perfectly flat on a table, despite their curves, as the last two images hopefully suggest, so they can all be joined together with little to no distortion.

2 These are the flat patterns that create the primitives to their left, if their ends are brought together flush.

3 The dark lines in column 2 are the "core" edges that remain the same after the variations suggested in column 3 are done, thereby preserving the primitive overall shapes. The partial cone pattern in the second row indicates how primitives are often merged or only applied to parts of a pattern.

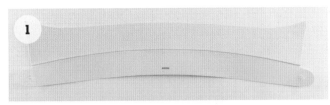

1

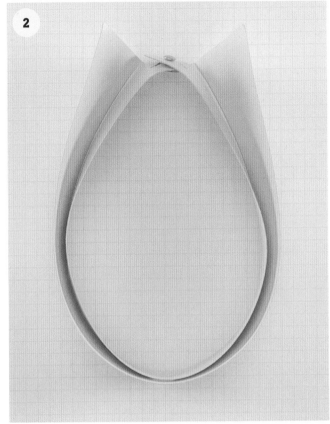

2

3

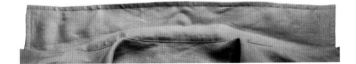

4

Pictured at left is a related marvel of collar geometry: The Downward Curved Foldline. The collar at the top (1) is a single flat piece of thick paper manufactured into a detachable shirt collar by die-cutting the shape and scoring to create the curved foldline. When folded on the scoring and wrapped into a ring (2), the inner layer stands away from the outer layer, essential not only for sliding in a necktie on such a stiff thing but for wrapping this folded paper into a smooth ring at all, because of how the curve changes the lengths of the portions of the collar separated by the fold, making the inner layer sit shorter overall than the outer layer, regardless of the shapes at the edges. A curved seam in fabric acts very much like scoring on paper.

One of the things that distinguishes tailoring from shirtmaking, is how basic it is in tailoring to stretch and mold the fabric so it does things that it wouldn't normally do, such as folding along a curved edge. Tailors make this happen, on fabrics like wool that will allow it, by bending a fold into a curve by stretching the outer edges while pressing, as in the photo (3) at left. Because it was stretched, this wool collar will no longer lie flat when unfolded, unlike the downward curved piece which won't lay flat when folded on its curve.

Without scoring, seaming, or stretching, it's quite difficult to create a consistent curved foldline in fabric . . . except that's what tends to happen naturally when you wear a convertible or camp collar shirt open: A soft roll line forms and it's a downward curve, as you can see on this normally flat one-piece, rectangular cotton collar after it's been worn open, at bottom left (4).

When shaping pattern pieces, mimicking or reinforcing what happens naturally when fabric tries to mold itself to the body is a basic strategy one sees over and over in the history of costume, and many standard collar shapes are good examples.

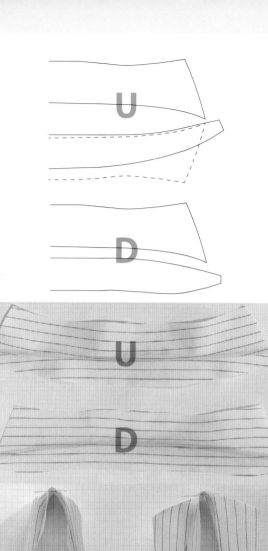

Applied to real collars, these geometries work themselves out in predictable, but potentially surprising, ways.

In the examples on these two pages I've used the identical collar shape, but attached it to two different stand shapes commonly found on traditional stand/collar shirts and in drafts for them, one that curves upward like the tailored wool collar on the previous page, and one that curves down like the paper collar. Note that the curves where the collars meet the stands are also identical, and thus parallel, except that for the D (down) version they're parallel when the collar is flat and open, while the U (up) curves match when the collar is folded over the stand.

In fabric, seamed, laid flat and open, the U version ripples, and D doesn't, as expected. When folded and wrapped end to end, notice again the dramatic spreading apart of the two layers—the nested cones—in the front thirds of the D collar, which is where the downward curve appears. The middle third of both collar and stand is a rectangle, with no curves, in both examples. The U layers stay pressed together tightly except right at the front, about which more later. Most significantly, both collars sit flat against the table when joined.

I'm calling this the most significant result because, as you can see when the collars are on the form at right, there's almost no way to tell which is which, precisely as a result of how all these curves flatten out when converted into cylinders and cones around the neck, as we saw in the primitives illustrations. In other words, the stand curve seems to have had, practically, no impact on the appearance of the two collars. In fact, as you can see in the far right column, both collars seem to curve downwards along their top edges when seen from the shoulder.

Nonetheless, the real differences between them are still there. Comparing the two front views at top right, note how the D version stands away from the neck all around, since its stand is inherently less of a cone shape than the U version's. In the two shots below that, I've allowed both stands in front to follow their natural tendency to pivot downward at the button/pin (as the blue lines show), bringing more of a cone shape to both collars, which almost completely erases any distinction between them . . . until you look at each from the side instead of head on, in the two lowest images. Notice how from this vantage, you can clearly see that the U collar is still being forced back against the stand, as it always was, while the D collar is still pushing outward away from the stand layer behind it, as it always was. Note, in the far-right U examples, how you can even see the stand through the collar, because of how closely pressed together they are.

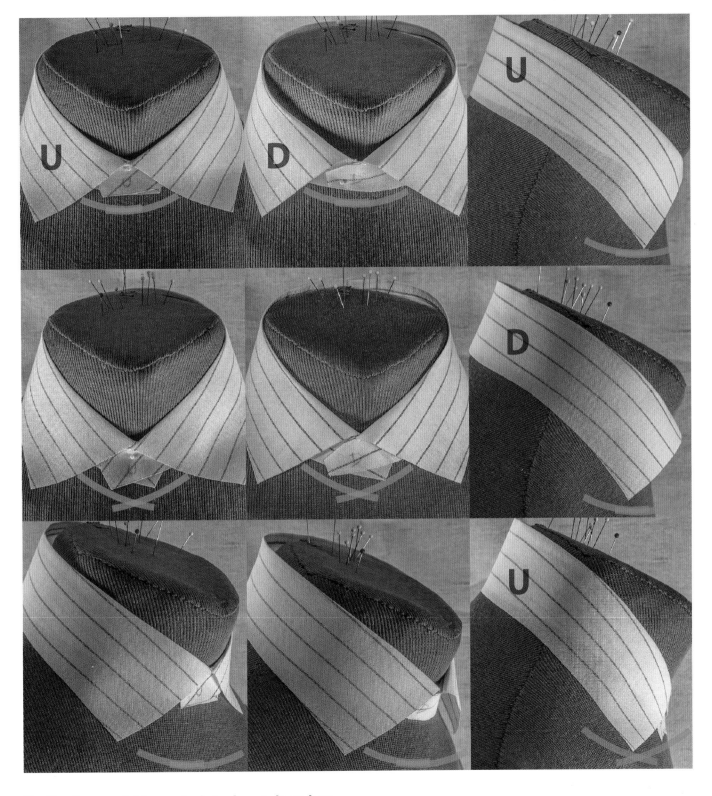

The blue lines overlaid on each photo above indicate how
the stand ends are arranged in each case at the center-front
button/pin; either parallel or pivoted.

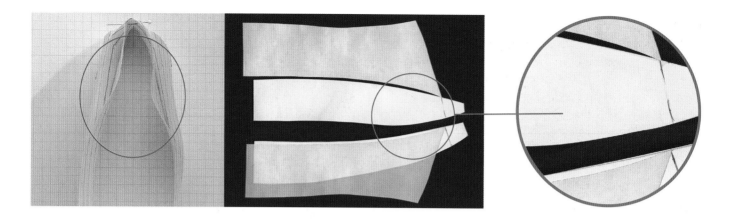

Collar/Stand Spring

We noted previously how, even though it's tight against it every-where else, right at the front of the Up example on the previous page, the stand does pull away slightly from the collar; here it is again, top left. That's the result of a tiny difference in curve, built into the collar's stand-seam edge, right at the front. As shown in the pattern scans in the middle above and mentioned previously, the collar and stand curves are parallel and identical, but you can see in the zoom-in that in the inch or so coming right off the center-front, the collar curve gets just a tiny bit tighter, and that extra curve is just enough to create the space you see between the Up collar and stand in that same area.

Old-time collar designers called this little extra curve "spring," a term generally in use by tailors, too, for any slight extra length or curve difference cut into a pattern or detail to give it some barely visible but still perceptible wiggle room or a better appearance. Collar

spring can be any amount or placement of curve difference that makes the collar's seam edge more deeply curved, however slightly or obviously, than the stand edge it'll join. It's clearly less needed or even noticed on the curved fold of the Down shapes from the previous spread, but it's there all the same, because I put it there, on both examples, as advised in my old collar drafting manuals.

Note that the collar's free styled edge can be shaped in all sorts of different ways for the visual effect wanted, making it longer or shorter as needed for different point shapes with little to no effect on how closely the collar wraps against the stand. Look at the test below , and you'll see how the slightly curved edge of the upper example, which is otherwise identical to the lower example, is all it takes to both introduce a ripple into the unfolded collar piece, and to push it away from the stand below when folded over it. Note that it's a curve *difference* between the two edges, not either's specific curve, that makes the real difference.

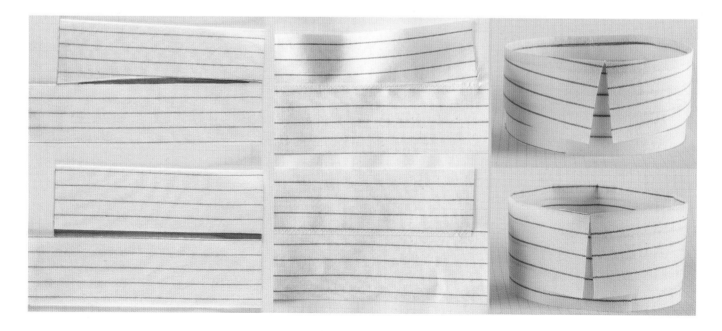

Center-Front Pivot

Finally, you'll have noticed all the emphasis I've been placing on how the stand ends cross, or are adjusted to cross, at the center-front. From here on I'll call this the center-front pivot. It occurs more or less in all not-too-tight collars with a single button at the center-front, but it can be stopped with an extra button, as in the collar ends shown at far right. The lower holes are for a separate collar stud, around which pivoting would be easy if the added button didn't put a stop to that.

This tiny room for up-and-down movement—apparently only extending from the button and hole in front out to the stand ends—is important because it's naturally amplified, in a lever-like fashion, back along the entire front of the collar/stand unit. This alters the stand's inherent cylindrical or conical cut, as long as the stand itself isn't so tight as to eliminate it. It's also a natural bit of comfort assurance, which for many may be the only reason to give it more than a moment's glance. But if you're designing collars, it's an issue.

The close-up black-and-white scans at right show the same stand. Look at the different angles (in green) that the stand takes just beyond the center-front band, depending on whether it's the shirt front lying flat (top) or the stand (bottom). This is the result of the stand being straighter than the neckline where they meet in front, which you'll recall makes it sit up like a cone to the shirt front's plate. But when buttoned, if the collar is not too tight, the stand end tends to straighten out, pushing the front band into a little fold just below it, as you can see in color at far right. Generally, this is a good thing, adding flex and comfort when the collar is buttoned, because it lets the collar move from cylinder to cone as needed at the Adam's apple. If you wanted to reduce or eliminate this flex without adding an extra button, you'd either (1) let the neckline continue downward across the band as the stand does naturally instead of forcing it up into a right angle to the band as it crosses it, as indicated by the orange lines below, or (2) reshape the stand ends as indicated by the yellow line above. I generally opt for more flex, but it's worth playing with.

The Bottom Line

The real drama in collar design mostly comes from the shape of the collar itself and not much at all from the stand shape. So, if you've got a collar/stand combo you really like, you can very probably get away with using the stand from it (maybe made taller or shorter as needed) with any sort of new collar shapes you want to try. If you start running into troubles, maybe the details here will help you sort them out. I hope so!

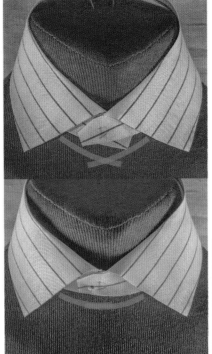

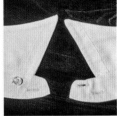

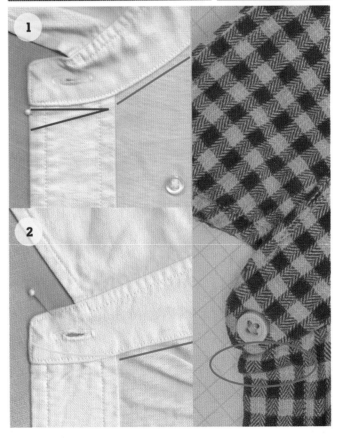

Dress Collar Profiles

Equestrian Collars

On the following few pages are a collection of bands, stands, and collars for which I'm providing a full-size pattern in the online content for this book, inspired by the actual garments pictured and discussed, or traced from the test collar experiments described. To simplify my descriptions, particularly in this section, I've invented a few new terms, defined here, that as far as I know are unique to me and this book, obvious as they may seem. They're all derived from the earlier discussions of collar geometry on pages 58–59 and are intended only to help connect those ideas and demonstrations with these actual garments and their shapes. Other terms already used and discussed there include "cone," "nested cone," "cylinder," "curved fold line," and "center-front pivot." If anybody knows of some other, more generally understood or commonly used terms for the same ideas, I'd love to hear about them. Thanks!

By "down," "straight," and "up" I refer to how the upper edge of the stand, the one that connects to the collar, is curved, as shown at right.

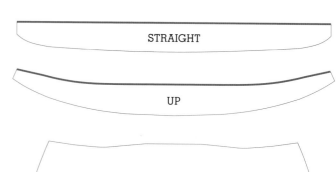

By "matched" I mean that the collar seam line is largely parallel to the stand edge it meets, either when coming together opened, as at top right (collar and stand can lie flat at the same time when open), or when folded over one another, as at lower right—in other words, just like the U and D collars on page 60 and 61.

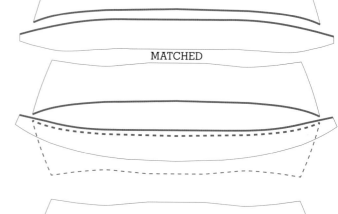

By "unmatched" I mean that there's a noticeable difference between the curves of the collar and the stand seam lines, which is obvious if the stand and collar can't lie flat at the same time either folded together or not without distortion.

By "high" and "low" I mean that the stand is either taller or lower than on an average shirt.

These classic band collars perfectly reflect the geometries laid out previously for cones and cylinders. I'm not sure what these variations found on women's "ratcatcher" riding shirts are called, but it's clear how they're made. The gray and white #1 collar is a pure cone all around. The two green images below it show a collar and the covering "stock" that came with it. Note how the #2 collar is curved only from the front back to a bit beyond the shoulder seam, then it straightens out as many collars do, across the back of the neck. The #3 stack that closes with hook-and-loop tape on top of it does the same thing, but because it closes in back the straight sections are at the ends, not the middle. Note also how the curve

for this layer is tighter to give it room—curve difference—to cover the band beneath it.

Also note the scanned images of the flat collar shapes provided here. These demonstrate the best way I've currently found to take a quick but accurate digital "tracing" from a garment or detail. Sometimes it works to just lay the garment section on the scanner and close it, but this usually results in distortions that can make the outline useless for tracing or cutting out later. If you instead carefully pin the section needed to a small padded board, such as I made for detail pressing at my sewing machine (also shown on page 48), then wrap and pin the excess material to the back of the board, scanning becomes trouble-free and truly useful.

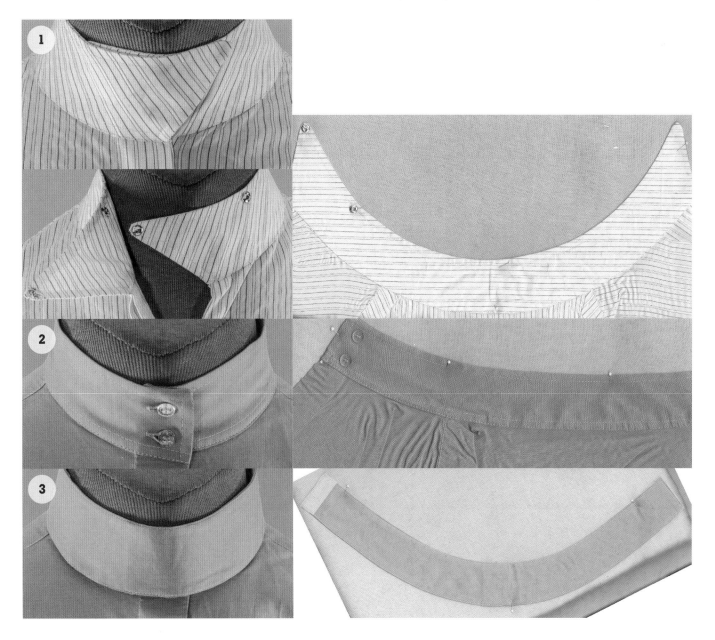

Dress Collar Profiles

Wing Collars 🖨

Although you probably don't wear one of these often, exploring how their pattern shapes work on the neck is an excellent place to begin analyzing fold-over dress-shirt collars because these are simpler than the standard dress-shirt collar on a stand and therefore reveal more readily the geometric behaviors they share. Below are four simple variations on the most common flavor for these formal collars these days: wings that extend back nearly to or even beyond the shoulder or yoke line, which makes them even more subject to curving-fold behavior than their early- to mid-twentieth-century predecessors. Those did all their folding in the first few inches around the center-front, and thus barely curved at all.

In each example grouping below except for #3, the first column shows the stand ends aligned for the cylinder effect described on page 58, and the second column shows the center-fronts pivoted to cross for the cone effect described on page 63. All are built on the same core band shape, with a straight upper edge and a gently upward-curved lower edge in the front neckline area. The variations are all in the wing shapes and angles; the band ends were varied just out of curiosity and have no significant impact on the collar appearance or behavior.

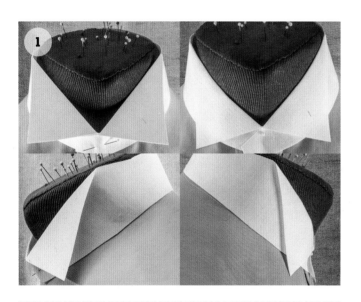

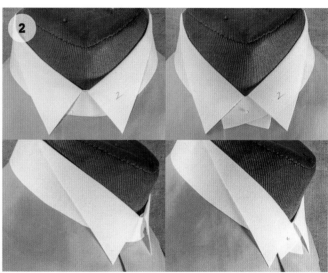

1. Note that when the collar isn't tight against the neck (left column) the wing fold remains straight and the wings can extend away from the collar, but when collapsed into a cone (right column) the fold is curved around the neck and the wings flatten against it.

2. When the wings extend back farther, the folds curve and the wings flatten whether the band is cylindrical or conical in front.

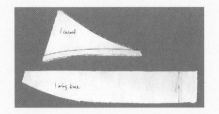

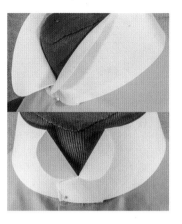

2c. To allow the wings to extend away from the neck regardless of whether the fold is long or the collar close, add the wing as a separate piece with a curved seam line.

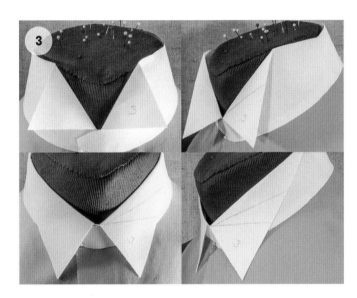

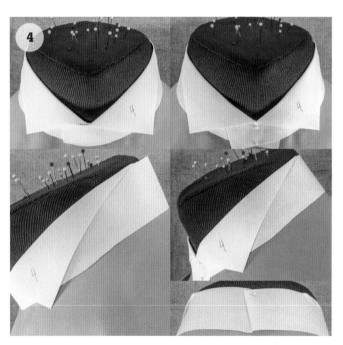

3. The angle of the wing fold is generally independent of the wing shaping. Each of the four designs on this spread could be folded at various angles as shown above.

4. Changing the band's center-front pivot doesn't change the shape at the back. To make the band hug the back of the neck (right column) you need to add a curve or an angle at the center-back.

Dress Collar Profiles

Here is most of my collection of vintage and contemporary manufactured detachable collars. Note that all are clear Downs, if I can apply the term to the one-piece ones (1, 2, and 4 below), which don't have a separate stand. But they DO each have a woven-in downward-curving fold line, even if subtle. Note that these are also single-layered, with just a binding around the edges to finish them, and are labeled not to be starched. Example 3 below and all the others are both two-piece and double-layered with slightly unmatched collars, obvious because of how they all buckle at least a little when forced flat, as I've done here. Also, these all have a longer and differently shaped stand end on the overlap end, each designed to limit center-front pivot. Any of these collar or stand shapes could easily be adapted to an attached collar or band or paired with a differently shaped stand.

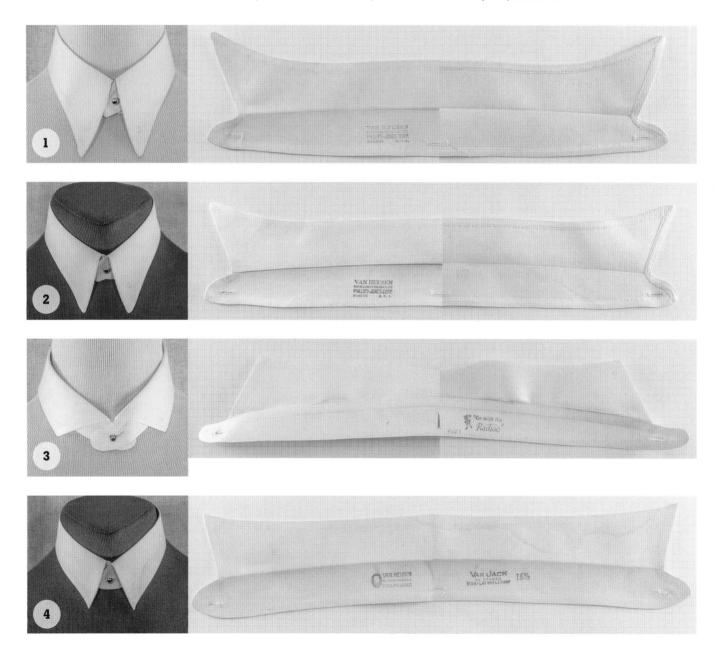

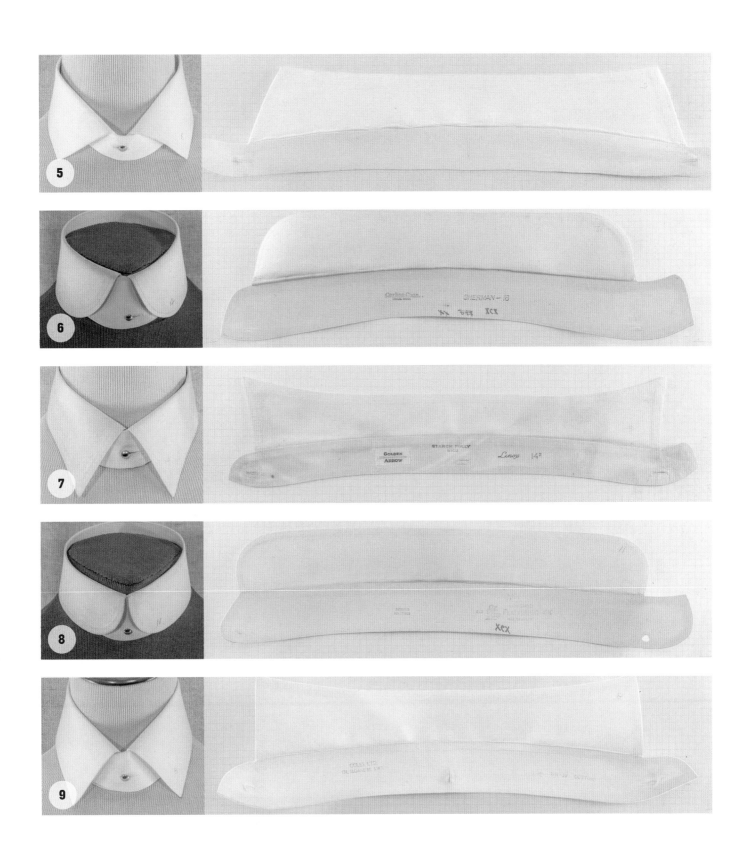

Roger Gray Men's Collar (below)

Down, matched: Both collar and stand lie flat together, because the seams that join them are the same shape.

Note:

- The collar edge's distinctive curve at the center back, allowing it to dip further below the neckline there than at the top of the shoulders
- The pronounced and consistent upward convexity of the stand top
- The slight upward turn at the stand's lower front edges
- How the collar's front edges have become slightly different through wear and ironing; choose one when copying, or make two versions

Turnbull & Asser Women's Collar (right)

Straight, unmatched: The stand and collar can only lie flat independently of each other, because the seams that join them are shaped differently.

Note:

- The distinctive, perhaps trademark, shaping of the stand ends beyond the collar edges
- The minimal shaping of the entire stand and collar; both are nearly pure rectangles, except at the ends
- How the collar's edge is very slightly curved lower at the center back, like the Roger Gray collar

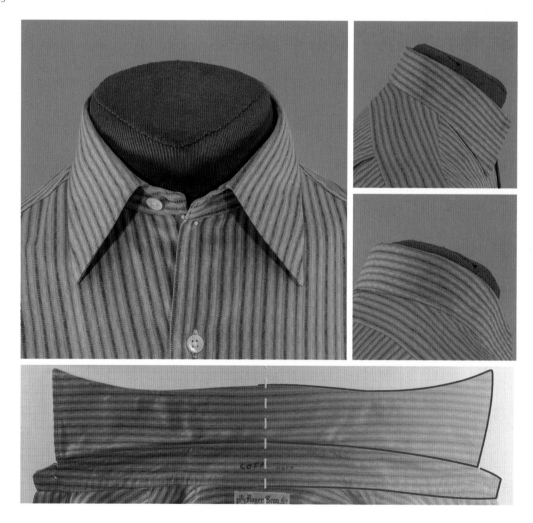

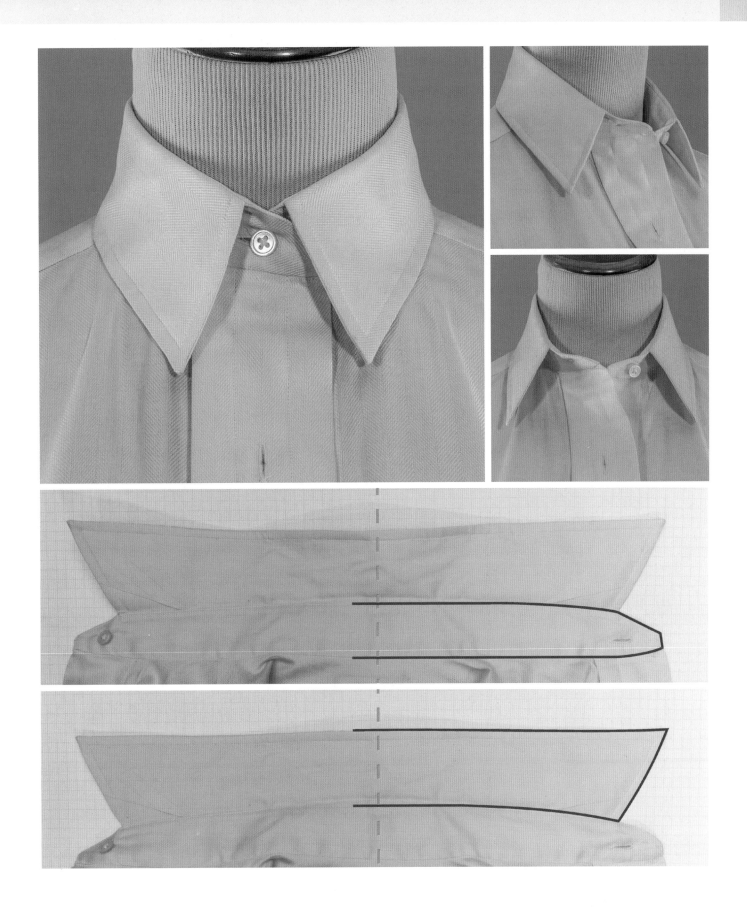

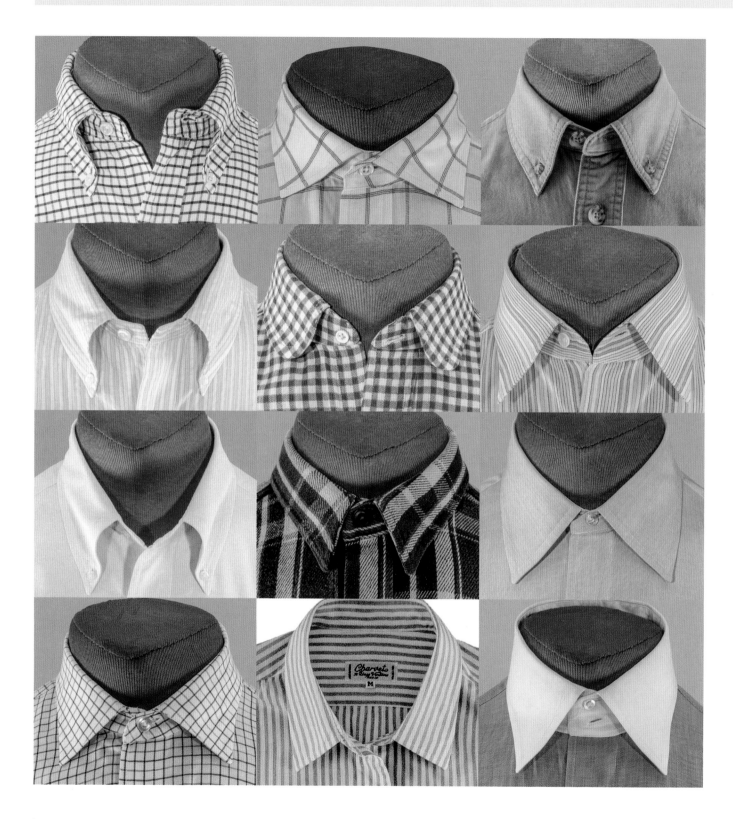

Draped and Drafted Collars 🖶

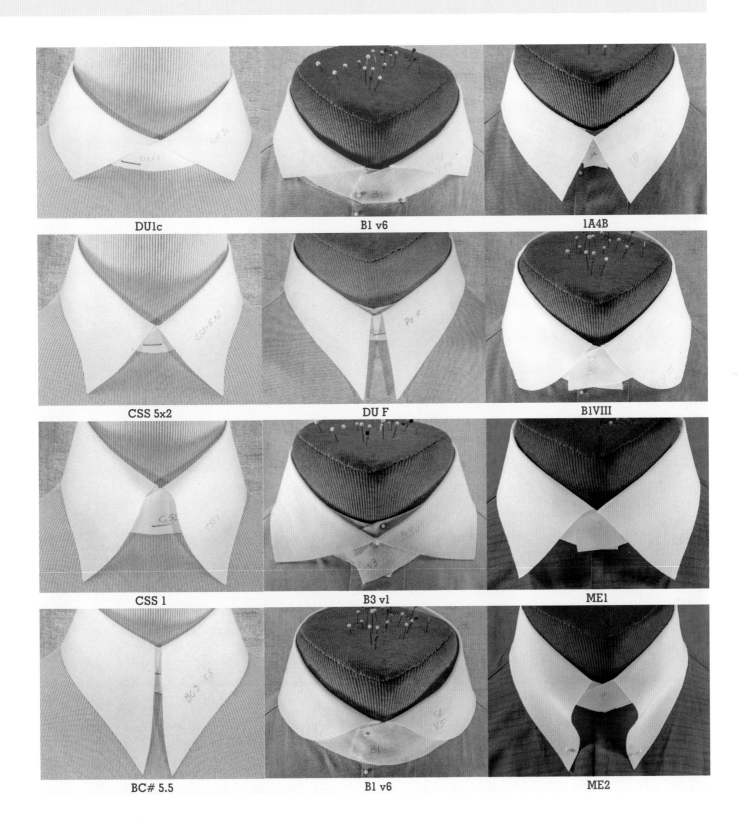

DU1c

B1 v6

1A4B

CSS 5x2

DU F

B1VIII

CSS 1

B3 v1

ME1

BC# 5.5

B1 v6

ME2

ANNA G.

HAND MADE IN ITALY

Anna Gorbatenko

When I stumbled upon Anna G's shirtmaking atelier online last year, I was simultaneously awed and humbled, thinking that here was an artist-sewer I'd wish had written a shirtmaking book! You may imagine how surprised and pleased I was to discover complimentary links at her site to my first book, which I took as an invitation to write her immediately. I've been picking her brain ever since, as you can see in her wonderful collar-making tutorial described on page 47, and I hope to have more interviews/tutorials with her to come at my blog, as well as on her own sites. Trained in fashion and textile design in Italy, Anna worked as a chief designer in the children's ready-to-wear company Sissy Missy before launching her shirtmaking venture with garments such as those on the facing page and top right, in which exquisite hand-stitching features as inspiringly as her apparently laser-guided machine topstitching. Of her miraculous cuff curves, she says, "For topstitching I use the felling foot again (see collar tutorial). The curved lines are challenging for all of us. I also pivot, as you advised. But slowly. Sometimes I stop every stitch." May I someday follow my own advice so well.

Book of Men's Shirts, by Shimazaki Ryuichiro. A Japanese sewing book, in Japanese, but still of great interest because the diagrams (as with all Japanese sewing books) are very useful, and full-size pattern sheets are included. It's a fine collection of contemporary shirt-detail patterns.

Cool Couture, by Kenneth King. This book, written by Fashion Institute of Technology professor Kenneth King, contains the best information on piping and piped pockets you'll find anywhere, along with tons of other fascinating, unique techniques, as one would expect from Kenneth.

Off-the-cuff-style.blogspot.com | Pam Erny's Off the Cuff website is a source for both great shirtmaking tips and tutorials and access to some of the best interfacings home sewers can buy today, at the companion site www.fashionsewingsupply.com, created by Pam in conjunction with interfacing manufacturers for the garment industry to her exact preferences as a custom shirtmaker; guaranteed not to shrink!

Cutterandtailor.com | Search "making shirts" for links to detailed, well-illustrated forum threads on shirt construction, high-resolution scans of old shirtmaking manuals, and a lot of informed chat; it's a fabulous site.

Malepatternboldness.blogspot.com |
Peter Lappin's blog Male Pattern Boldness
(Best. Blog. Name. Ever.) pretty much sets
the bar for shirt-sewing sew-alongs, mean-
ing they're extensive, well photographed,
and clearly described, with active comments and replies. He's even taken a shirtmaking class at FIT in New York and shared
his experiences in detail. Don't miss it.

Grainlinestudio.com | Jennifer Beeman's
site is both a pattern line and a source
for equally wonderful sew-along blog
posts, many in support of her much-loved
Archer women's shirt pattern, an obvious
candidate for block-ifying.

Mike Maldonado | When you're ready to
get hard-core with making shirts, simply
hook up with Mike Maldonado, a career
old-school custom shirtmaker, who has
put together a massive video curriculum
on every aspect of making shirts and making a living doing it. It's expensive at $400
but priceless if you want to really see a pro
doing, and explaining, every bit of it, from
pattern drafting and fitting to stitching up
the smallest details like pin-bar holes and
tab collars. Separate modules from the
complete course are available, too, and
access to Mike via email is always included.
And for readers here, he's even offering a
large collection of exclusive clips to down-
load. You'll find all Mike's links online.

GRAINLINE STUDIO

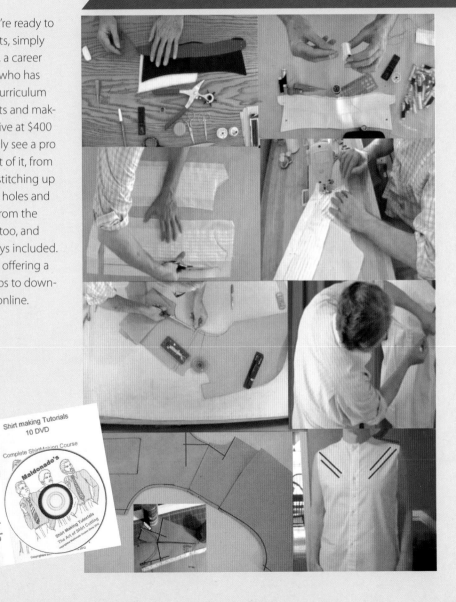

To Consider

Here are my results from an exercise you might enjoy if you're feeling the call from your inner Shirt Collar Nerd. The idea was to skip all existing garment-derived collars I had and go right to the drawing board with simple geometry and some precise incremental pattern changes, to see what I might learn. As usual, it seems to be all about subtlety with collar shapes, but why bother if you're not also about that? The smallest of these shapes feels in line with the current impulse I detect in contemporary shirts to both start from scratch and to scale down the proportions, but of course you could start anywhere. I didn't get beyond the shortest of the stand options I drafted out at bottom left, but all my patterns are online for you to do with what you will. Definitely draw up your own starting points to learn the most.

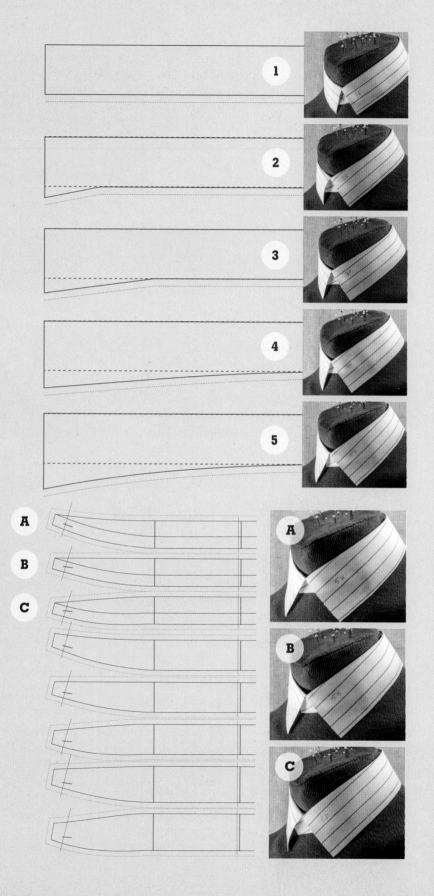

Vintage Dress Shirt Features

In the early 1990s, I had a once-in-lifetime opportunity to get into the archives at the Metropolitan Museum's Costume Institute, with a (pre-digital) camera. Below are some shots from that memorable day, upgraded as well as possible from my old slides, and with great appreciation to the Met for letting me reproduce them here.

The top two are from the all-custom wardrobe of the Duke of Windsor (note the royal monogram), the others are from unidentified donors. I'm struck by the pointing upward sleeve angle and chest-covering facing at bottom left, the between-the-legs extension and horizontal pleats at lower right (definitely a men's formal shirt), and the trove of vintage details on the ducal garb.

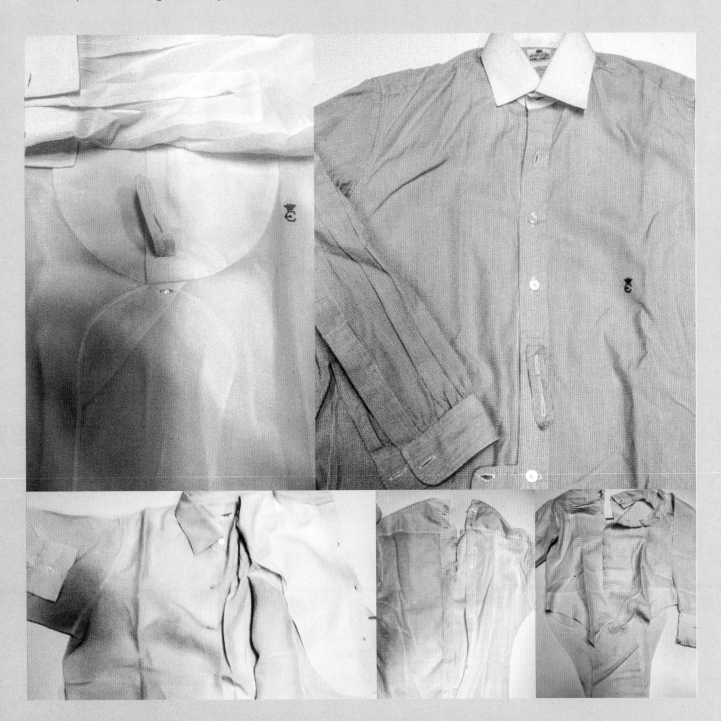

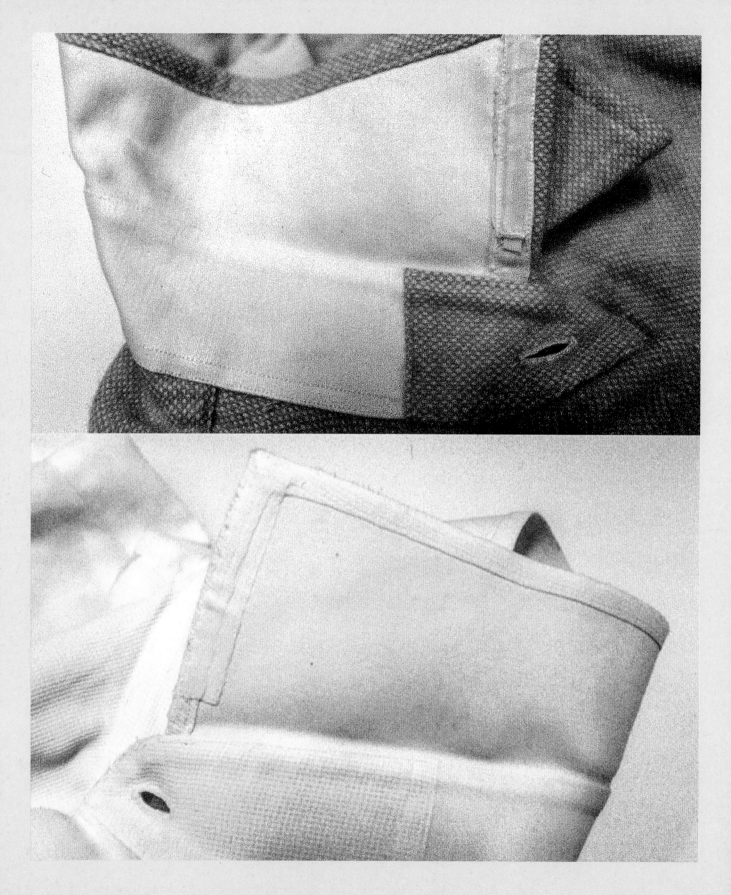

Ditch the Undercollar? Why Not?

If you found the no-undercollar shirt collars (and barely-covered stands) at left in a vintage shop, I suspect you'd assume that some kind of cost-savings was behind the idea. But these are how ALL the Duke of Windsor's collars I saw at the Met were assembled, so I think we can scratch economy as the motive. Reducing bulk seems more likely, especially given the heavy canvas each collar is built on. I love the concept of simply wrapping fashion fabric around a carefully cut stiff foundation, as opposed to turning a double-layer bag as expected. It's my preferred way of shaping any small detail in heavy fabric or with sharp corners that would be a nightmare to turn well, like the triangular-tipped belt loops below, shaped and secured with glue-stick and a thin fusible. It also brings to mind the oft-seen bound edges on detachable collars, the way many tailored undercollars have raw edges like my heavy tweed topcoat (*Threads* #38, Dec 1992) at mid-right, and also the fascinating practice of 50's-era designer Davidow whose unlined and turned-under once and triple-topstitched raw edges were signatures of his high-end women's suits, at top left below. Below his is my version (*Threads* #60, Sept 1995), digitally darkened so you can see the raw edges better.

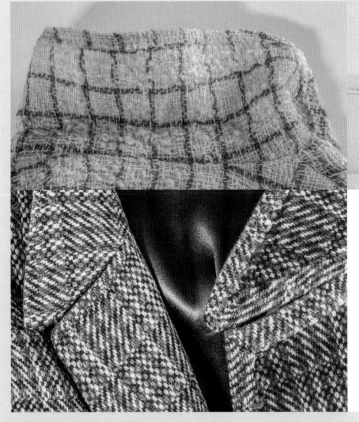

CHAPTER 4

The Sport/Work (or Loose-Fitting) Shirt Block

The Sport Shirt

Garments of this type commonly include shirts suitable for informal, leisure, sport, or outdoor-work activities, such as hunting, fishing, gardening, and the like, plus classic styles, including Hawaiian and guayabera. Of course, the details described here can do equally well on shirts and blouses worn for work and other more formal occasions. What I'm calling a sport or work shirt commonly has these features:

Fit

The rectangular bodies are unshaped at the sides, underarms, and yoke so they fit the figure loosely, and can be comfortably, but by no means necessarily, worn over other not-so-loose garments, such as dress shirts, T-shirts, turtlenecks (all the smaller shirt blocks), and as over-layers, smocks, or coveralls above complete outfits. They can be the same size as a dress-shirt block at the shoulders, sleeves, and armholes and simply without side- and underarm-seam shaping; or larger in all these places, with the same shoulder slope as a draped dress shirt; or with shoulders not matched to your body, but left as is from a copied garment or trusted pattern that feels good. Flatter sleeve caps and/or less deep armholes are often found on more sporty shirts compared to dress shirts, and are very effective motion enhancers, as are shoulders that are slightly less sloped than the body underneath. Typically, the neckline will also be slightly to considerably looser than a dress shirt's, and may or may not be intended to close at the throat.

Details

Any kind of collar, or none, can be found on sport and work shirts, but I'll use this chapter to focus on collars without stands, including those called "camp" or "convertible" collars, collars with cut-on stands, and collars cut in one with a facing, as well as necklines with no collars. Facings themselves are characteristic of these shirts and come along with the sort of collars I'll be discussing. Yokes are typical, and are larger than dress-shirt yokes if present, but many of these garments are without a yoke. Sport shirts can have short or long sleeves, and if long, will have loose-fitting cuffs or facings or simply be hemmed, either long enough to cover layers underneath or intentionally shortened to reveal them. Cuffs and plackets are common, but simple facings and otherwise hemmed sleeves are, too. Pockets are rarely left off these garments and may be multiple and at both chest and hip level, especially if oriented to utility. Hems are likely to be square or straight, intended for wearing out, rather than shaped for tucking in, as on typical dress shirts.

Fabrics

Fabrics are woven, more likely than not to be medium-weight, crisp or soft, and certainly washable, but also suited to heavier or tough-surface fabrics like canvas or denim. These garments range from gauzy single-layer summer-wear or even pajamas to all-season outerwear.

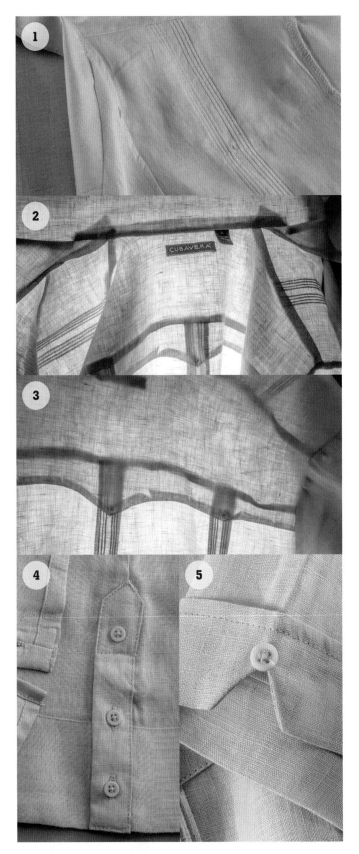

While a quick image search indicates that guayabera shirts are as likely to have two-piece collars as one-piece, here's an example with a simple convertible collar and facing. Made from a light-weight linen, it's totally free of interfacing. The facing is relatively narrow and ends right at the start of the inner yoke's front edge, (1, 2), near which point the upper-collar's neckline edge is clipped and pressed under to finish the collar on the inside back. The facing's inner edge is simply serged and pressed under once, then topstitched. Note how the signature vertical rows of alforzas (fine, tiny pleats) sewed closely together are delivered in two different ways: in front and on each pocket, the pleats are made of the front or pocket fabric directly before cutting out the pattern pieces. In back, each of the three strips is separate and appliquéd onto the garment fabric as a premade decoration, no doubt after cutting the back. The one-piece inner yoke is a bog-standard unshaped piece like those found on ordinary dress and sport shirts, about 3 inches (7.5 cm) deep at the armholes and 4 inches (10 cm) deep at the CB, whose front edge is slightly forward of the shoulder line. Over it, the one-piece outer yoke is shaped front and back, extending between 1 and 2 inches (2.5 and 5 cm) below the inner yoke edge in back and about 5 inches (12.5 cm) down the shirt front. The neckline and armscyes are the only edges it shares with the inner yoke. Directions for forming the notch at the short-sleeve hem are online, and the button strips at each side are the overlap part of an on-seam placket detailed online, with the underlap being simply the twice-folded-under side seam allowance. The outside hem facing and the pocket tops are identically formed uneven bindings, stitched first about ½ inch (1.3 cm) deep on the inside, then wrapped to the front and topstitched after being formed into the characteristic gentle points as needed.

Garments Profiled Online:

Author-made linen blouse

Christan Dior men's raw silk camp shirt

On the next several pages I show a variety of collar and outer-edge shapes and let them each reveal their qualities together on the form. But because the back half of each of my test collars is pretty much a simple rectangle, I noticed no difference in how the backs of the collars behaved, despite the neckline edges in front being different. Even the front differences were usually quite subtle, if visible at all. So I did another series of tests with more extreme edge differences, which I'll show next.

In each of these first combined tests, I cut all the collars the same neckline length, based on a slightly lowered version of my dress-block neckline and with the collar ends intended to meet when the center-fronts of the Center-Front & Neckline module I used here overlapped. I cut the module fronts with a cut-on facing, and set the CFs at about 1 inch (2.5 cm) in from the folded front edges.

This is a little deeper than most would likely want on a shirt, but I was thinking about the shape of the notch between the collar end and center-front edge when the collars were worn open, and I didn't want that to be as small as the Guayabera shown on page 84; I was going for jacket-like here. I decided a perfectly rectangular collar shape would be a good baseline to start with, and so it proved, I think. All the shots below and at right are the same collar simply converted into different shapes by varying degrees of openness and sometimes by folding the free edges to simulate reshaping. I also sometimes tried the same collar "muslin" on my female form, which has a slightly smaller neckline and much different posture than my custom form, to see how a lowered, larger neckline would look.

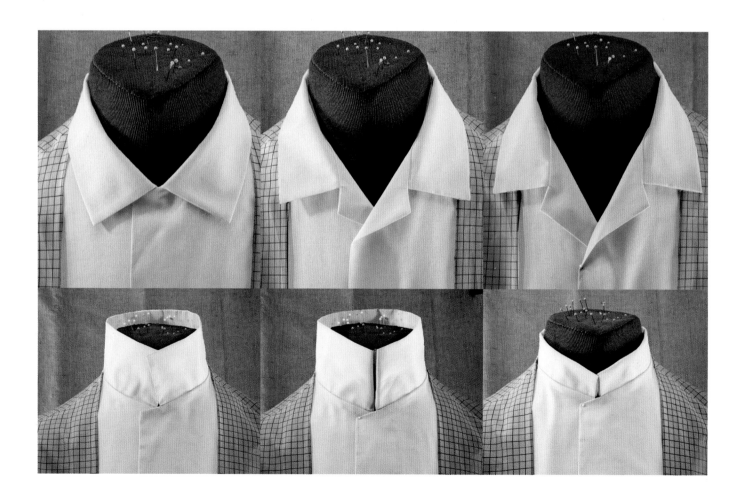

PATTERN rect

The three shapes below (including the rectangular collar, again at bottom for comparison) differ only in the shaping in front of the neckline edge, and show almost no differences when on the form. Note how pattern 1's collar points stand slightly away from the body when viewed from the side and how pattern 2's collar shows pronounced wrinkles at the neckline when buttoned in front and unfolded, due to its extra height exactly there.

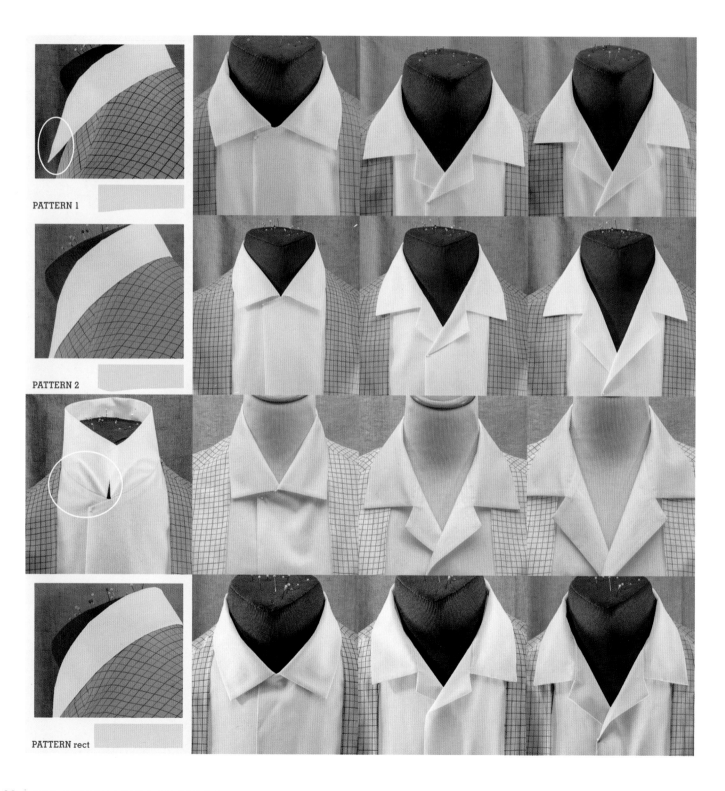

PATTERN 1

PATTERN 2

PATTERN rect

Pattern 3 is pattern 2 with an angled front edge and slightly deeper neckline curve. The long points on patterns 5 and 4 are at slightly different angles, and I believe the way 4 presses close against the body when open wide (third image) compared to 5 below it, and vice versa when opened less widely (second image), may be the result of 4's more deeply curved neckline shaping compared to 5's.

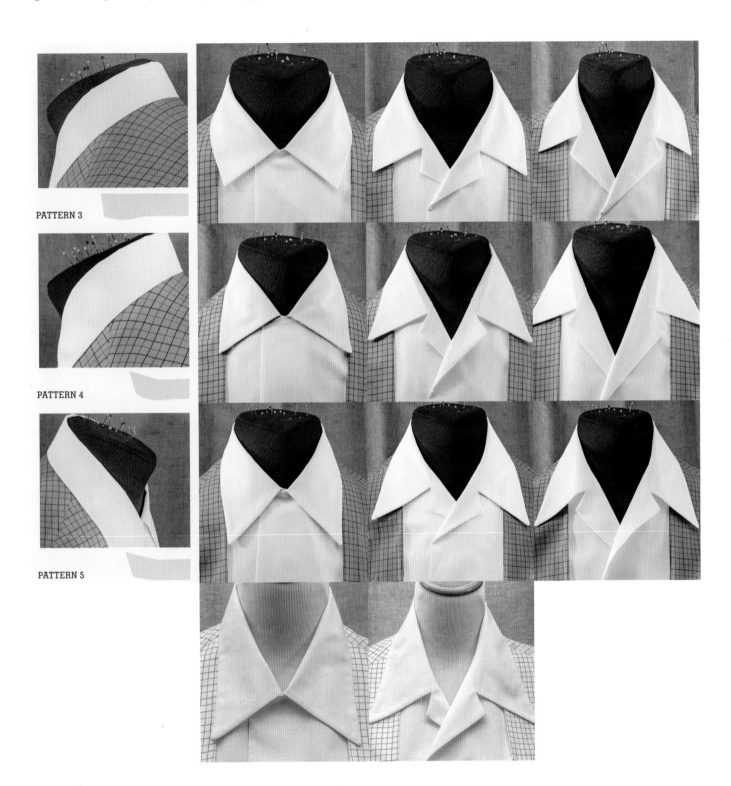

PATTERN 3

PATTERN 4

PATTERN 5

Pattern 6 results from trimming another largely rectangular pattern so its front free edge height makes a more equalized notch with the width of the fronts beyond the collar, which could of course be done with any collar shape for a more jacket-lapel-like appearance.

Patterns 7 and 8 share essentially the same neck-edge shaping, and pattern 9 is the same as pattern 5 along the same edge.

PATTERN 6

PATTERN 7

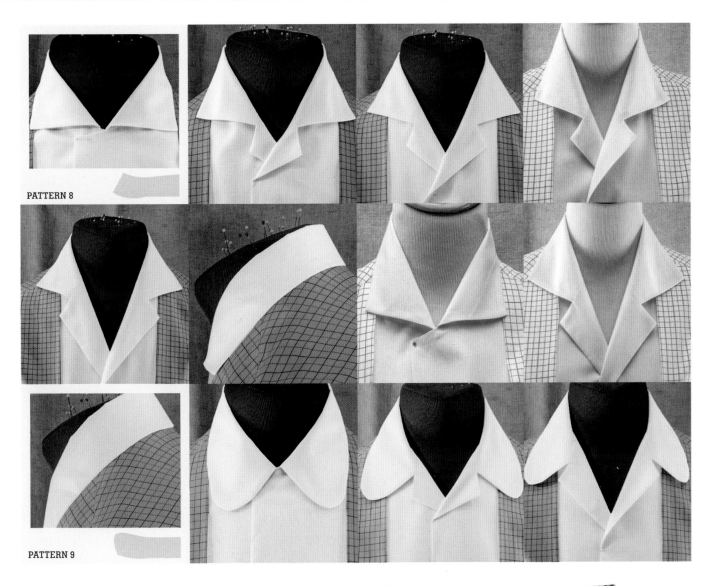

PATTERN 8

PATTERN 9

Christian Dior men's silk camp shirt: This collar seems to be a very subtle pattern 2/3, if not an angle-ended rectangle.

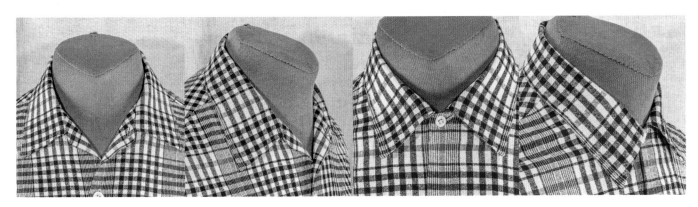

Featured Patterns

V-Neck Convertible Collars

In the midst of my convertible-collar explorations, I was pleased to find in my pattern collection what I'm guessing is a 1980s-era sport shirt with a lowered neckline featuring a convertible collar. I wondered what kind of core shapes it employed, and the answer is below: the collar's neckline edge has a downward curve like Pattern #1 from page 88 for a not-lowered neckline. Subsequent research has shown that upward curves and straight edges are just as likely to be used on lowered and V-necklines, but the downward curve certainly makes sense here, possibly because the lowered neckline itself has a downward curve when viewed from the side (unlike, for instance, the dress-shirt neckline, which is more or less straight from the side, as discussed and shown in the Dress Block chapter, pages 56–70).

Comparing this dropped neckline with the one on the Center-Front & Neckline module I'd been using for the convertible collars so far, at bottom left below, you can see it's just a straightening out of the curve into a diagonal to the CF, then a horizontal jog to create the lapping width to the facing fold, creating a distinct V-neckline. Right next to the diagram is the old pattern converted to a Center-Front & Neckline sub block, and in the photos below and at the top of the next page, it's on the forms, with a few variations from folding and reshaping.

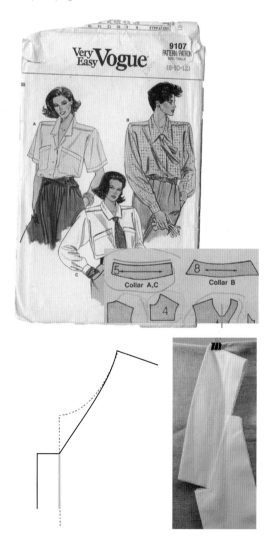

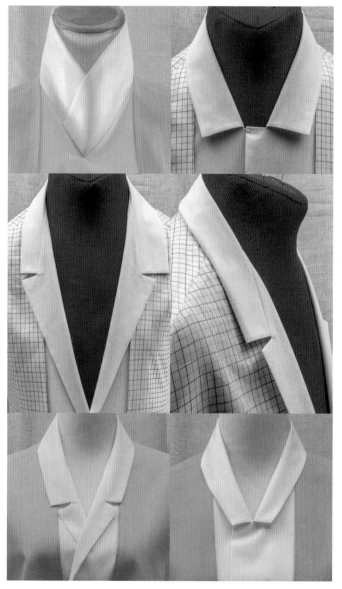

One-Layer V-Neck Collars

Wanting to speed up my explorations, I switched from two-layer collar muslins to a single layer in a heavier muslin fabric with a little sizing added, and for some reason decided to try a collar shape that didn't extend all the way to the center-front of the same V-shape. I was delighted with the Evil Queen result below, pure Disney fairy tale to my eye.

Featured Patterns

Here is a progression of reshaped one-piece collars that explore the idea at the heart of the Evil Queen shape: a "convertible"-applied collar with a roll or fold line that doesn't extend onto the front; in other words, a collar with a cut-on stand, attached with a neckline facing. These were each trimmed down from the preceding shape; it makes sense to start oversized when you're intending to make a series of test cuts to reshape a muslin collar.

As you can see, these "stand-and-fall" shapes started out with a smooth front edge, which quickly evolved to have different shaped ends for the stand portion and the fall portion. This gravitates back toward dress-collar shapes, which of course is only one possibility, but a compelling one for me at least, and one I'll pursue further as we progress.

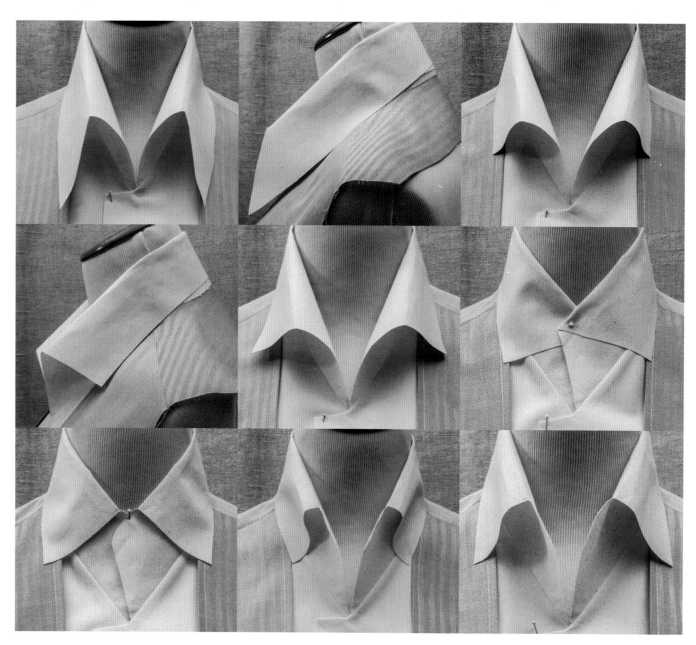

No-Notch U-Neckline

The next step that seemed natural to explore was to move the collar ends out to the full extent of the neckline, beyond the center-fronts, eliminating the notched-lapel effect that all these collars have so far potentially had when opened at the neck. At the same time I decided to convert the V-neck to a deep U-curve to facilitate the sewing. Dropping the curve ends helped, as you can see in the last two rows.

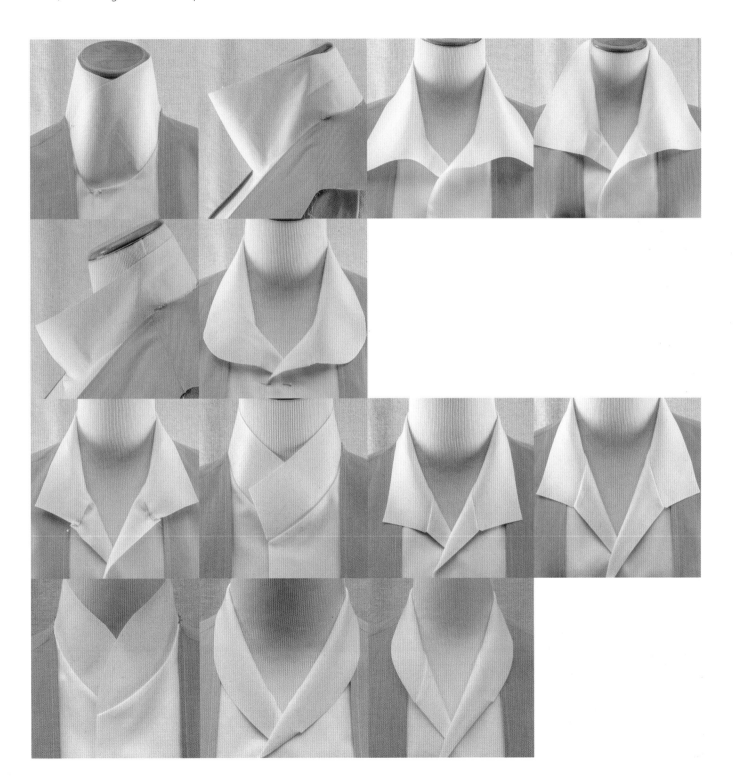

Featured Designer

Michael Cepress

The menswear collections, fashion exhibits, and theatrical costumes of Seattle-based designer and college instructor Michael Cepress have been featured and pictured in the *New York Times*, *Fiberarts Magazine*, *DANCE Magazine*, Seattle Magazine, and *Seattle Metropolitan*, and displayed in U.S. and European museums. Yet despite two degrees in fine art and textiles, as a clothing maker, he had to undertake his own training. Michael generously took time out for an email "interview" which continues online.

What initially inspired you to start garment making?

"As an art student working with textiles and fibers as my medium, I soon came to realize that one of the most powerful ways we can communicate with these materials that I love so much is by using them on the body. I love spending countless hours with my materials, so learning to sew was an obstacle and challenge that I wholeheartedly welcomed. While in art school I worked from commercial patterns for a short while, but quickly felt the itch to branch out and make my own. The minute I left graduate school I found work with the Seattle Opera, where I was able to work with expert tailors and dressmakers day in and day out. American theaters are one of very few places where ages-old sewing traditions and techniques are still used and celebrated, so I knew that it was essential for me to be there for a time. My sewing know-how is absolutely essential to my work and process as a designer, and I am certain the work I do would not be as strong if I were not so enthralled by the careful nuances of expert tailoring and sewing."

"I've never taken a formal fashion design class, never taken a sewing class, and never been taught patterning or drafting or any of that stuff. I'm more or less self-taught in that regard, which was a grueling and kind of awful way to do it."

Featured Patterns

Combination, or Italian, Collars

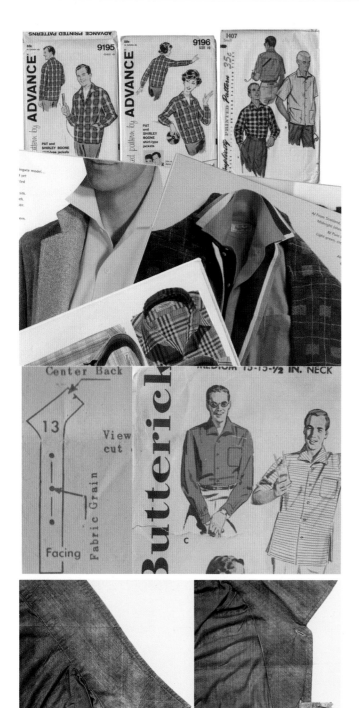

Anybody familiar with vintage shirt and jacket patterns has no doubt come across collar and lapel shapes like those at left. But unless you've opened them up, or seen the sort of garments they produce, you may not quite get what's going on with them. I certainly hadn't until I spotted a colleague wearing the shirt I eventually managed to Xerox at bottom left. What I noticed was simply that on an otherwise apparently normal shirt, there were no seams between the collar, the stand, or even the fronts, on the inside of the collar anyway, which was worn open. Up close, I saw the under-collar seam on the garment right side, but the top collar was cut in one with the facing, as in the pattern-piece diagram at far left, so it was indeed seamless on that layer, very like a shawl collar, in fact, except for the under-collar behind it. Instead, it's a sort of combination of shawl and convertible collar shapes, hence the term I've chosen for it.

Judging by the number of 1940s- and 1950s-era patterns for this combination sort of collar I've by now seen and sometimes bought, it must once have been quite popular, but it's certainly no longer common, which is a shame considering how versatile, not to mention clever, it is. By no means limited to shirts and blouses, it's essentially a tweak of the more familiar shawl collar setup, shown in diagram #1, at right, in which both the upper and the under-collars are cut in one with the garment or facing below them. The areas I've circled in the diagram show the problems with it: the sharply angled seam line where the under-collar joins the neckline and the shoulder seam all in one go is challenging to sew cleanly and strongly, and the seam typically found at center-back on the upper-collar, where you'd generally prefer not to have a seam.

The combination's tricks shown in diagram #2, deal with both, first by separating the under-collar from the body so it can be sewn to the complete neckline after the front and back are joined in the usual way, and second by splitting the facing partway down the front, so the upper-collar and lapel part of it can be economically cut on the fold at center-back. The whole facing/collar could be cut this way, but the split makes it much easier to find room on a fabric layout. Also, cut this way, the front facings are on the bias, which you may not want all the way to the hem but is great to have at the neckline and otherwise wouldn't have. In diagram #3 you can see at the dotted line how the same core structure can be adapted to almost any imaginable center-front and collar shape for which you'd like a seamless face, at least until you get to the facing seam, if you have one.

In diagram #4, there's a typical drafting process for creating such a collar from an existing neckline and a basic rectangular collar pattern to be reshaped as wanted later, which is probably the most straightforward way to do it. Notice that the angle between the lower edge of the collar rectangle and the center-front is determined by the depth of the neckline in relation to the shoulder seam corner, because here the collar pivots from the center-front until it meets the shoulder with a little overlap. The process works very well with different neckline depths, resulting in many possible collar/front angles, as shown in diagram #5 below. For this project, I wanted to be a little more free to play with the idea, so I've come up with some other ways for establishing this angle for a variety of results, as described on the following pages.

Every pattern I've ever seen for this collar structure on a shirt has the same, very basic shaping for it with a convertible-collar-like roll line and no neckline closure, as in 5 again, and the patterns opposite, while the actual shirts I've seen with it are all shaped slightly, as in the third image down in diagram #4, and in my photocopy, and the late-1990s Paul Stuart catalog pages reproduced at left. These all provide a fold-over roll line with a stand and fall, and a little simulated stand edge at the center-front overlap and a neckline button.

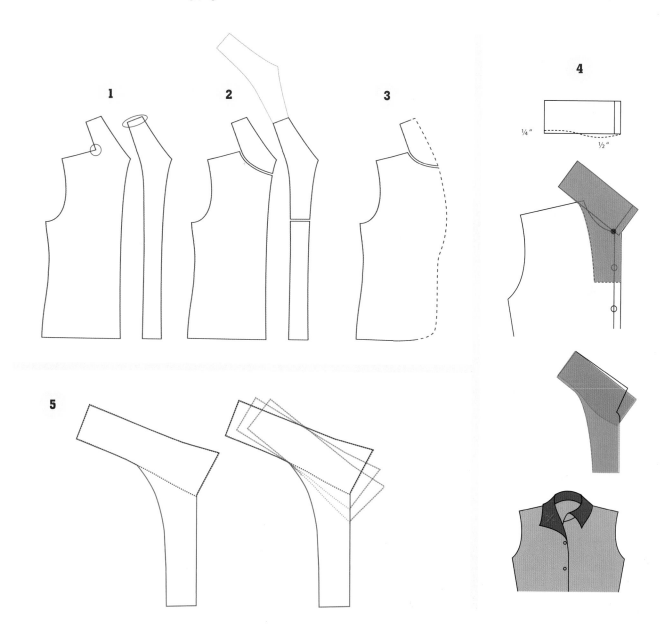

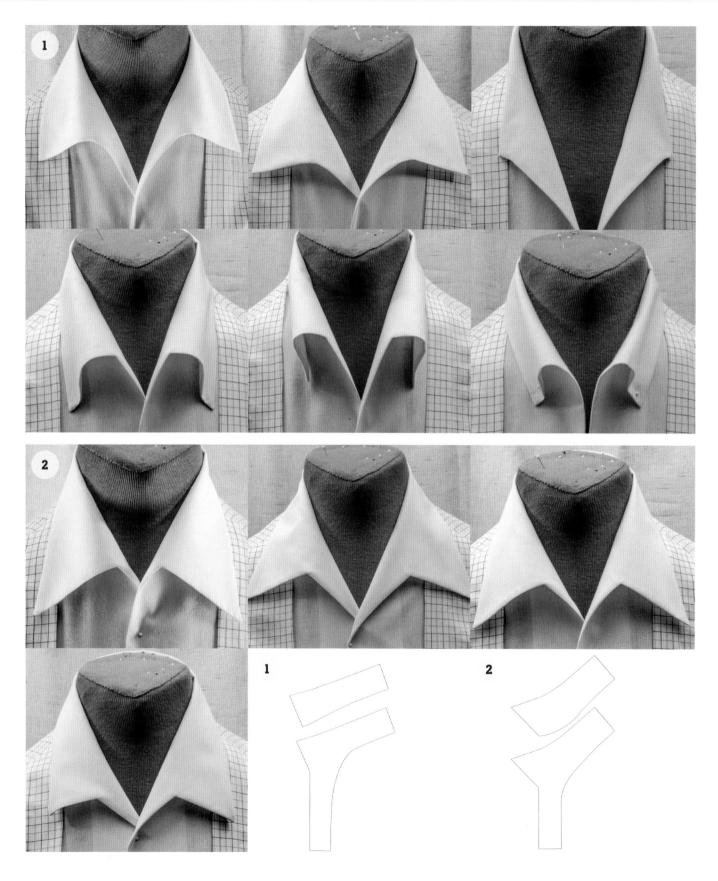

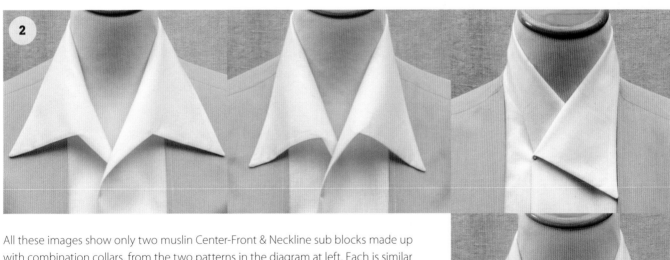

All these images show only two muslin Center-Front & Neckline sub blocks made up with combination collars, from the two patterns in the diagram at left. Each is similar to the typical shape offered in all the old patterns I've seen, here arranged opened, closed, and variously folded to display the range of even these basic shapes, which differ—however slightly—in the angles both at the collar points and between the facing portions and the collar portions, implying that they were built upon differing necklines. Here, I simply cut the collar portions to match the length of my default sport-block neckline (the same used for all the convertible collars) and stitched them to the existing curves, then let them fall as they would on these two different-sized necks, confident that block logic would allow me to easily convert these draped results into patterns.

Draping Neckline Position

Even though these collars are melded to their shirt fronts, we can still adjust their appearance and size quite well on the forms (or ourselves). In these images I've pinned out length at center-back of the muslins on the previous spread to raise the collar (and thus the neckline) to various positions on each form. Note that this also pulls the centers away from each other, decreasing the overlap, but that may be a good thing in some cases, and is easily corrected for if not.

At right are examples of the first step I'll take to merge any draped center-front & neckline sub block with a any block's shoulder and scye sub block when both have been arranged together on the form. As you can see, changing the collar length hasn't made it any more difficult to pin the sub blocks together or to lay them flat along the overlap, ready to transfer outlines and the under-collar's neckline to paper or master pattern tracing.

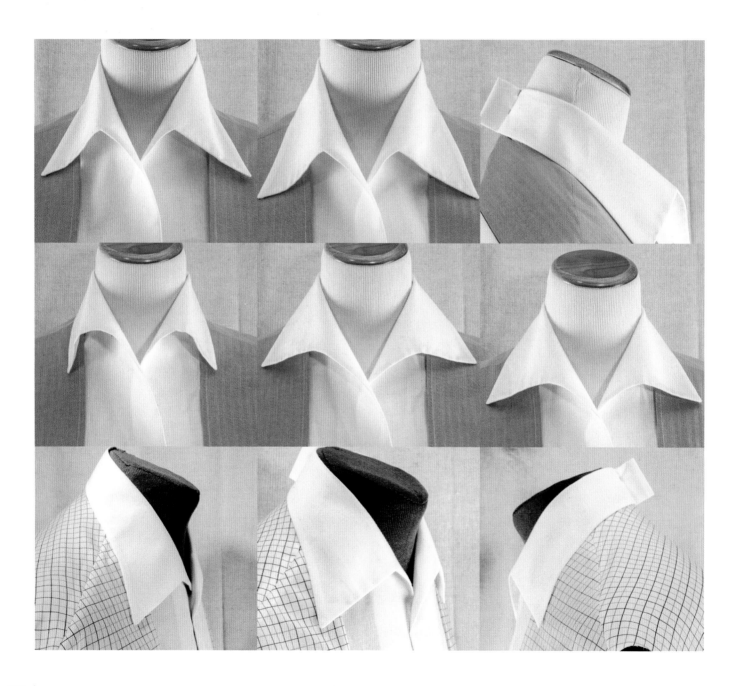

Sub Blocks from Form to Flat

You can either mark the relative positions of the modules (two upper images; the pins are alignment marks only, not joining anything) and then realign them off the form, or simply pin them together before taking them off, as below. If they were smoothly joined on the form along these simple edges, they'll go together flat as well, as designed.

Note that only the front neckline and center-fronts need be traced in these examples, to show their new relative positions and the neckline's shape from the combination pattern. The back neckline on the yoke and collar are only being checked for matching length; their shapes won't change.

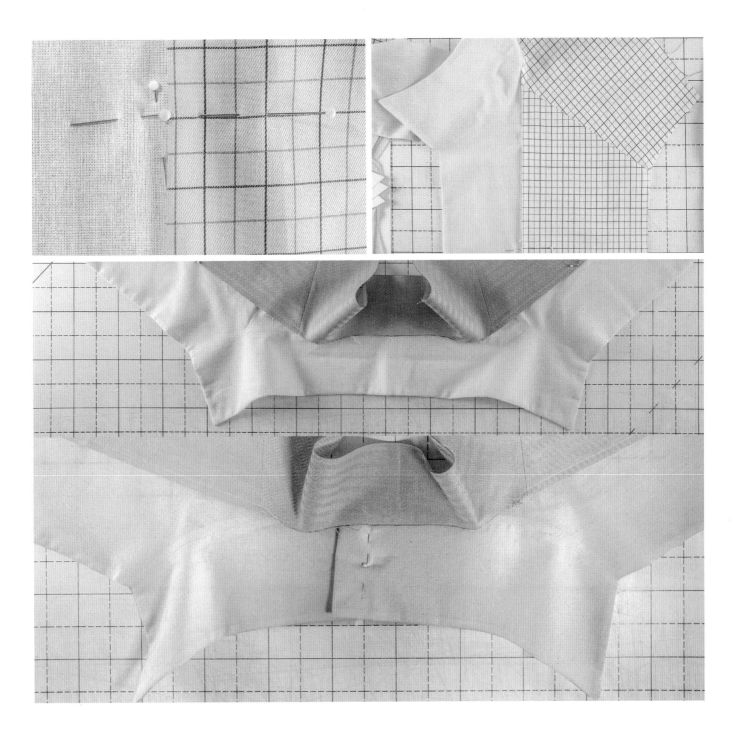

More on Neckline Position

The collar-to-facing angle experiments below highlight the draping approach. As an alternative to starting with a given neckline and tilting a collar to match it, you can simply set out a range of angles and place the same collar and facing shapes onto them, then drape the results to see what happens, as I've done here. This worked equally well on the smaller form after pinning length out of each muslin at the center-back. As expected, I liked all of them, so to establish a neckline shape for the under-collar of each one as set upon a particular block neck, I slipped my male and female dress-block full-neckline sub blocks (last seen in Stand or Band Draping in the Dress Block Chapter) over each muslin on each form, and traced the neckline edge from those onto the muslins.

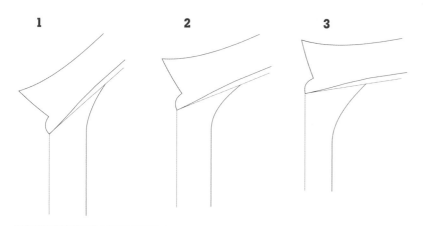

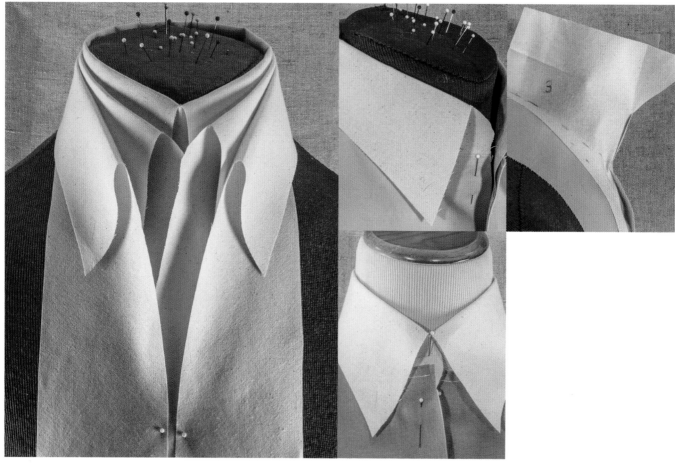

From Neckline Marks to Pattern

With the traced under-collar neckline marked on the collar muslin as described on the previous page, you could proceed directly to the shirt based on the block module used. Here's what I did to place the marked collar on a different block, with a lower, sportier neckline.

I first drew another neckline (yellow dots below left) on my muslin, about 1/2 inch (1.3 cm) below the transferred one (blue dots). With tracing paper over the muslin, I sketched in and then trued up a complete neckline following the yellow dots, dropped a front angle that looked slightly less extreme than the original drape I wanted, then added seam allowances. (I could have also found the front angle in the next step instead, by pivoting and sliding on the red dot I placed on the front pattern's neckline seam at the shoulder/yoke line.) I placed the tracing I'd just made over my existing front, aligning my re-drawn neckline with the neckline/shoulder-line intersection (the red dot again) and my collar front with the front's CF overlap, tracing the blue shape in the middle diagram onto the front to create its new raised neckline. For the under-collar's neckline, I drew a straight line from the red dot to the new neckline at the front in order to create some curve-difference (remember "spring" from dress-collar geometry, on page 62?) where the under-collar will meet the center-front, indicated in pink below. This is what's making this collar stand up from the shirt front, instead of lying on the same plane with it, as you can see it doing below, when the collar is complete.

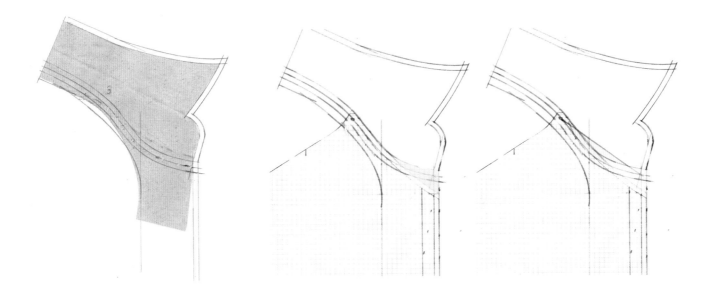

More on Collar/Body Spring

In the several drafts and patterns for these combination collars that I've explored, there's a clear disparity between those under-collar necklines that match the curve of the body neckline and those that don't, using flatter curves than the necklines they'll join. The greater the difference between the joining curves (or how much spring there is between them), the less able the joined pieces will be to lie flat on the same plane. In the four upper images directly below is a sample collar made with the sample's right-hand neckline cut with spring and its left one without. The flatness that results between collar and body on the no-spring side lets the sample lie flat on the table there, but

on the form, the front wrinkles from this flatness and is obviously a problem.

At near right are the neckline curves from the sample just described. The spring side was the deeper black curve and the no-spring side was the red line that matches the under-collar edge and the parallel edge of the front neckline below it. Note that I would have gotten the same no-spring results if I'd reshaped the collar edge to match the black curve, as indicated in pink.

Testing two different angles for the same collar shape, as shown in the lower group of photos below, it becomes clear that the need for spring between the under-collar and the body decreases the lower the collar ends dip down in front, reducing

the angle between the CF and the collar, as in image #1. Collars that lay flat against the chest don't need spring. Collars that sit closer to the neck, with greater angles to the CF, as in #2, do need it, as I've indicated with the red neckline curve there.

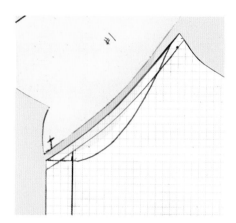

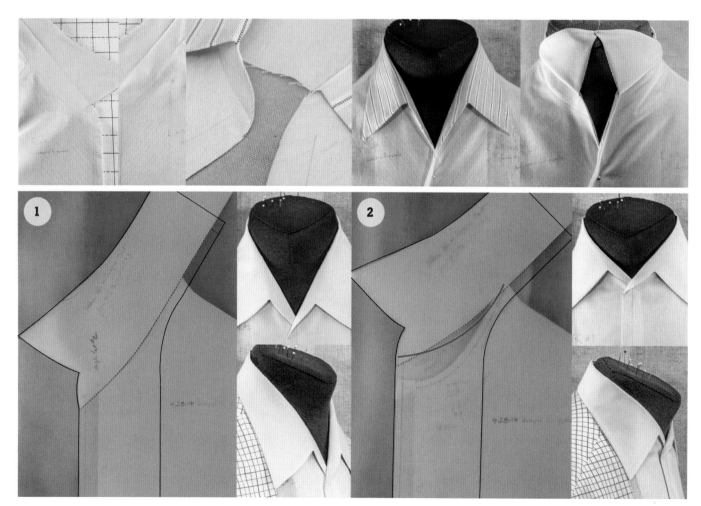

Combination Collar Construction

Unless you're up for a seam at the center-back, you can cut a combination collar-facing unit on the fold either on grain or cross-grain, with the results shown below if your fabric is striped or otherwise directional. The under-collar can also be cut on the fold, or flat, or on the bias with a hidden center-back seam. Press all the seams open when you attach this/these pieces. There's a full step-by-step illustrated sequence for constructing these neat collars online as usual.

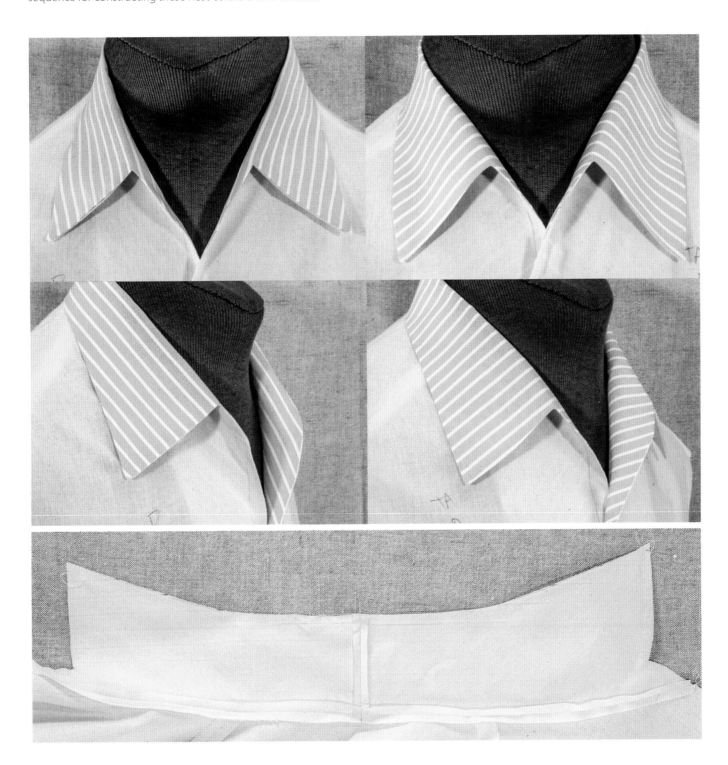

Featured Patterns

Combination Collar Shape Play

To facilitate further playing with these versatile shapes, I switched to single-layer muslins as before, cutting five distinctive upper-collar edges, then made a single, shaped cut to the front edges of each and re-draped. These will all transfer easily to a neckline block, as described in "Sub Blocks from Form to Flat" on page 103. More examples are available online.

1

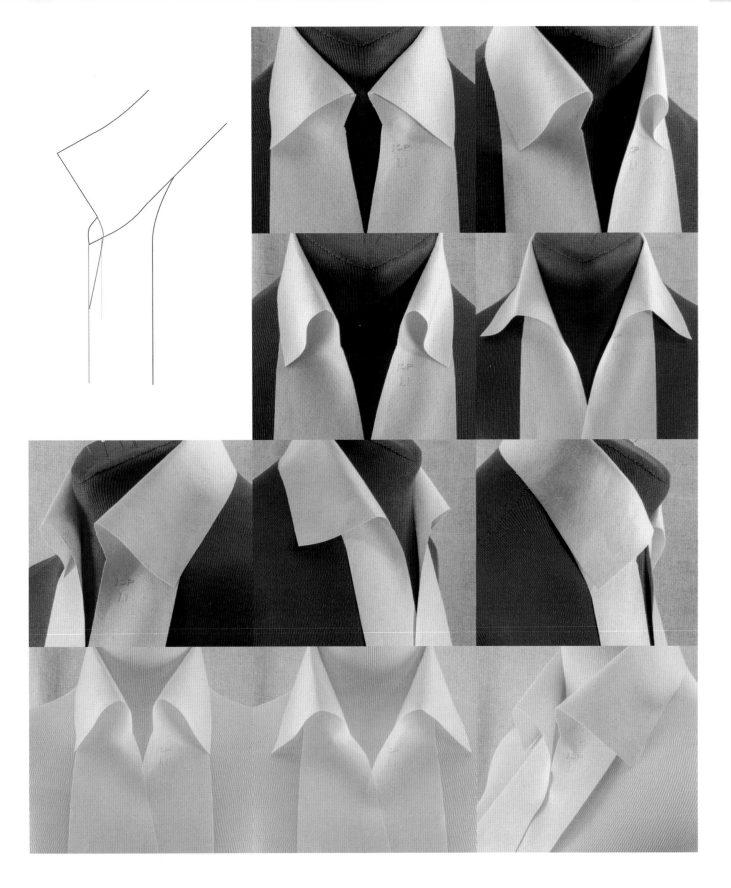

2

3

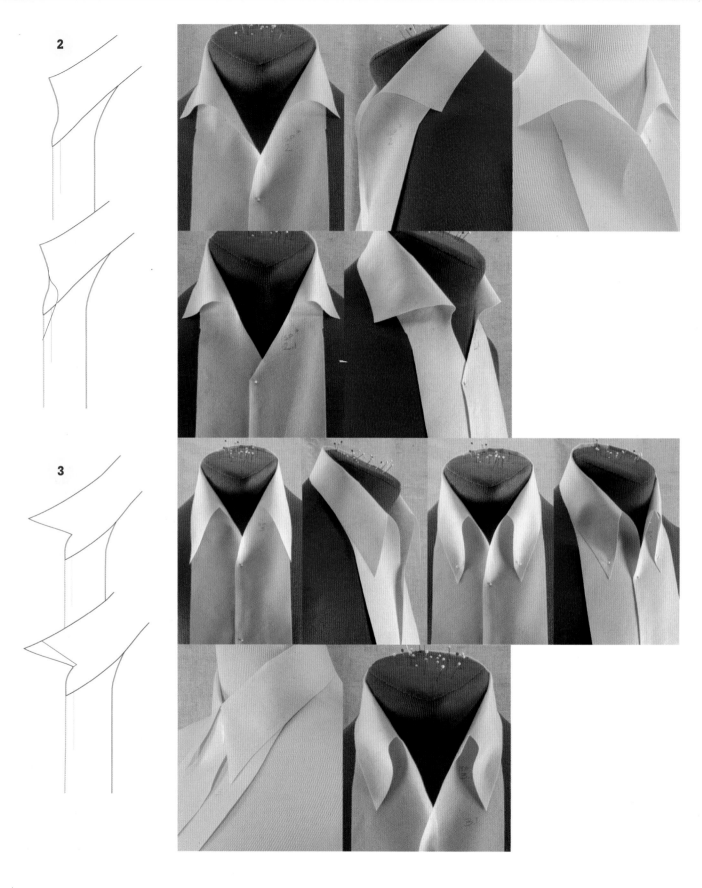

4

5

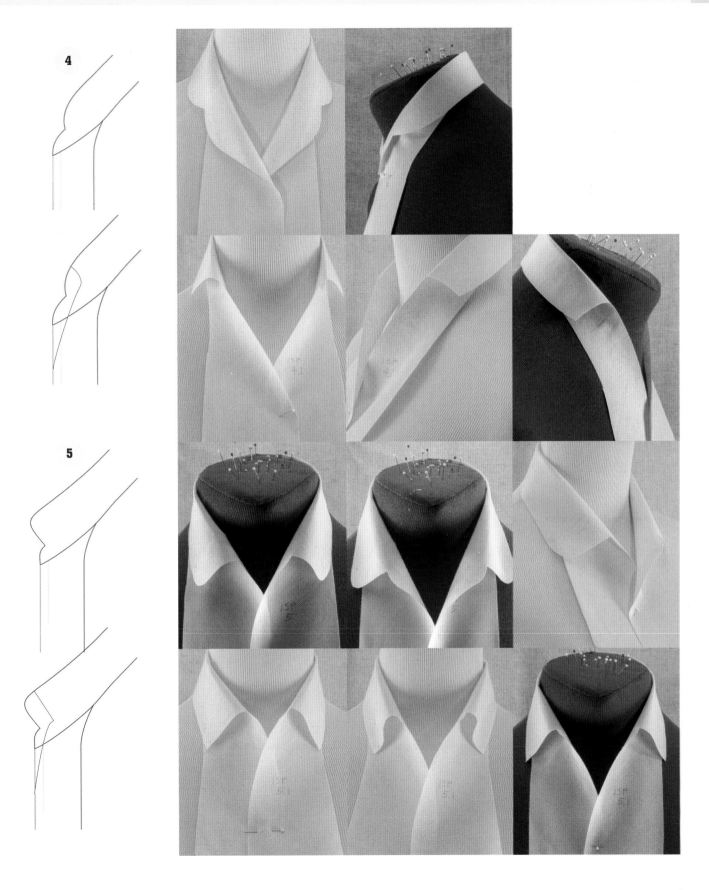

Featured Garment | Columbia Fishing/Sunblock Shirt

The mesh back and floating back panel very effectively air condition this lightweight shirt. At right you can see that a standard shoulder yoke has been shortened in back to a bit above the back neckline, splitting it into two single-layer epaulet-like shapes from which the mesh and the back panel fall. The panel is wider and deeper than the area it covers only by about 1 inch (2.5 cm), where it's secured at the underarm (even though it looks bigger than that), so it pushes away from the mesh even in the absence of a breeze. The mesh offers as much stretch as it does circulation.

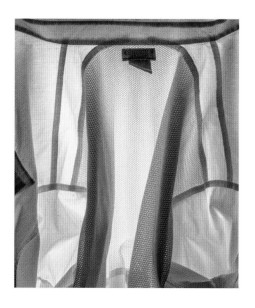

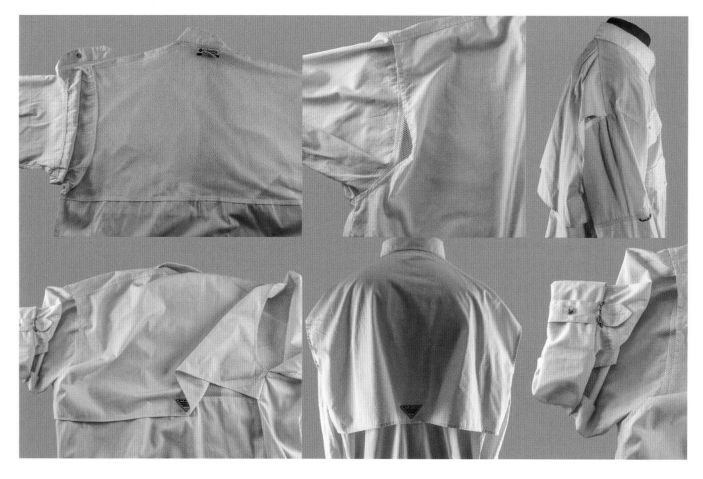

Garments Profiled Online:

WILLIS & GEIGER F-E TATTERSALL BUTTON-DOWN

F-E is short for Willis & Geiger's term "function-engineered," which refers to the deep shoulder pleats tacked at the waist, the underarm gussets, and the elbow darts, all of which are intended to allow for enhanced movement for the wearer of this wonderfully beefy, well-made shirt.

POINTER LOT 1225 COVERALL JACKET

This coverall is full of interesting details. Like the W&G, there's no yoke and a nonpieced pleat, but in every other way it's a more complex solution. Here the shoulder seam has been angled rather dramatically toward the back at the armhole.

DULUTH TRADING CO. F.O.M. SHIRT

Here's another shirt explicitly engineered for freedom of movement (F.O.M.), like W&G's F-E. It's got the same pintucked gussets as the W&G, but a deep yoke and carefully shaped and pieced inserts at the armholes in back in place of those simple pleats. The sleeve darts are gone.

Online Article: Bi-Swing Backs in Action

The simplest and smoothest looking way to ensure great freedom of arm movement is for it to fit closely, especially right at and just below the shoulder joint and the underarm, which is, after all, the body hinge that needs to be unrestricted for the arms to move with maximum freedom. When I compared a few shirts with extra details to enhance freedom of movement, the conclusion was obvious: Fitting well to start is still the main factor in a successful application, both for movement and for looks.

My wife's gardening coverall of choice for over twenty years, this much-loved shirt is finally looking like it's ready to retire, although a similarly lightweight canvas has proven elusive to this day; maybe on the remake I'll even try out the unusual bound seam allowances detailed at near right. The on-seam lower pockets, on side seams moved forward to put them in a more ergonomic position, were the main feature of interest until I finally tried on this XS-labeled garment and found it perfectly comfortable. It has great arm mobility, due to the almost capless sleeves and shallow armholes, which seem to completely neutralize the otherwise too-low yoke edge, which is right where it would normally create immovable resistance and render the small, also too-low pleats useless. But here they're working fine, and thus a new sport block is found for both of us, so nearly rectangular everywhere that a pattern is scarcely needed—just measurements. I'll definitely copy the simple sleeve-placket structure; it's just a self-faced, cut-on vent at the end of the back sleeve seam. Those pockets are simply double-layer rectangles from side seam to front with folded-under edges at the openings.

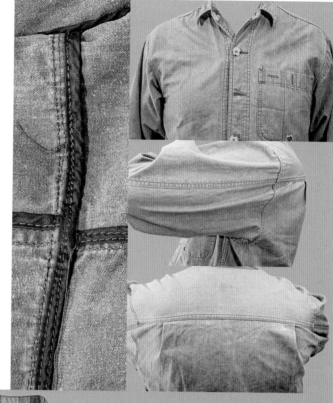

Same vintage, same simplicity, same bound seams, same shallow caps and armholes as the green S&H shirt, this collarless, snap-closing coverall gets even more wear—daily, in fact—for long stretches. The V-fronts are simply faced up to the yoke, where the topstitching continues across the dropped back neckline. The inverted back pleat is about 3 inches (7.6 cm) deep. The double-layer lower pockets are just about perfect, both for easy sewing and while in use, and are ideal for everything from shopping lists and tissues to pounds of wet beach pebbles, both at once, safely separated. These are simply joined and turned rectangles (the top layer has two 3/8-inch [1 cm] tucks along the bottom edge), with the open top edges both folded toward the garment. The inner edge is unfinished, topstitched to the garment and wide enough to support the snap diameter; the outer is finished and stitched to itself. The whole thing is double-stitched at the sides and bottom except at the side opening, which is stitched to match beforehand. I doubt my wife has ever used the upper pocket, but it's a perfect prototype for any shape or orientation of a welted shirt pocket. The ripples in the 1/2-inch (1.3 cm)-deep curved and rolled hem have come to seem an essential character feature instead of some kind of construction fail.

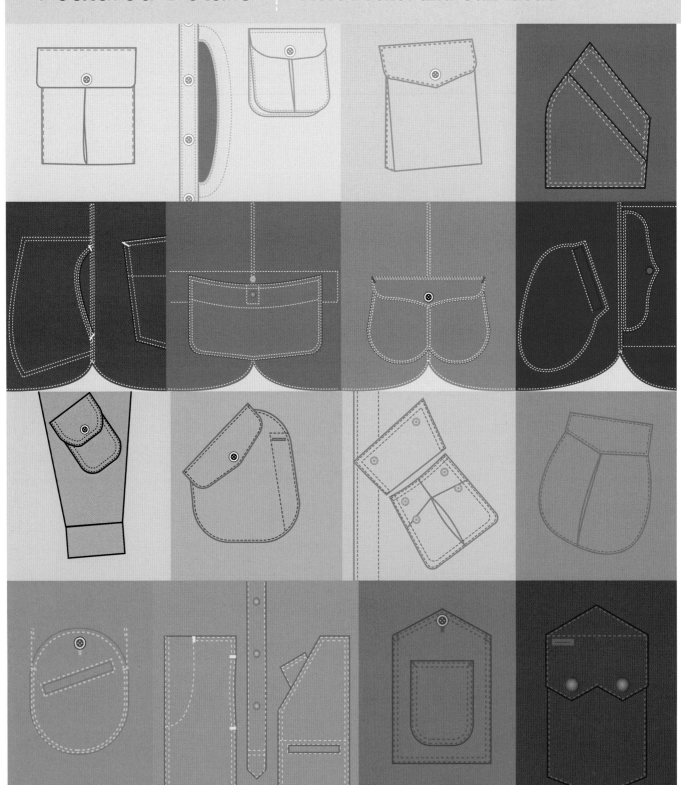

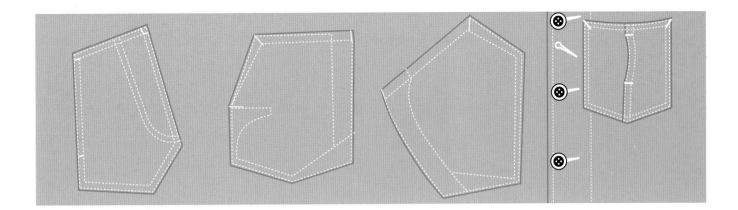

Thanks to the current enthusiasm for vintage worker's coats and shirts, and the endless space for images that is the Internet, there's no shortage of inspiration and the close-up photos to feed it. You'll find more on these and many other ideas on my Pinterest boards, and of course, many other boards packed with similar riches. Patch pockets are clearly the easiest to copy or draw upon, as well as the most easily suited to unlined shirts, but multiple layerings and through-all-layers topstitching to secure interior bags to the garment pretty much open the door to any kind of pocket you'd like to have. If you've wondered what odd-shaped and angled pockets like those above are—or were—for, it's likely to be a pocket watch on a chain. Nowadays, they serve well for

glasses. Custom-shaping a pocket for a favorite tool or device is a most satisfying way to flex your design instincts.

As for cuffs, a shaped vent-and-hem facing at the end of a seam is about as classic a work finish as you could wish for, and fraught with surprising options. The key thing here is to test to discover how best to precut the sleeve seams to allow for the transition from seam to vent edges, to which you'll stitch the shaped facing, which usually goes to the inside but could just as well turn to the outside. Patterns and directions for a few of these examples are online.

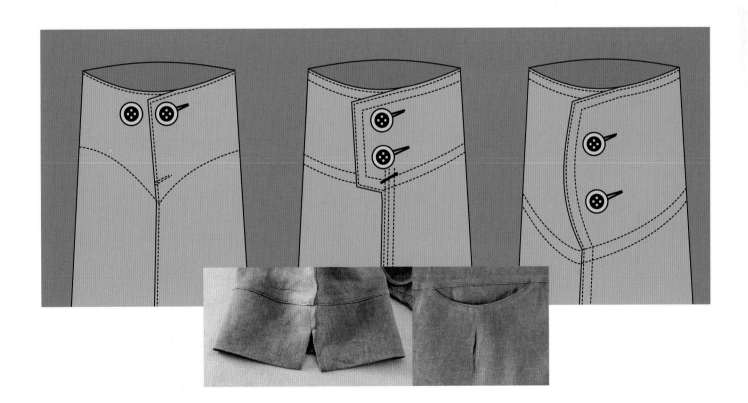

Mike Maldonado's separate offerings on convertible and combination (he calls them Italian) collars are the first tutorials I bought from him, and I found them excellent. He's much more about drafting basic versions and step-by-step construction in each one than I am here. If you liked his free clips that I mentioned earlier, then you'll probably enjoy these too, especially if you're interested in these styles. His convertible construction method is quite unique!

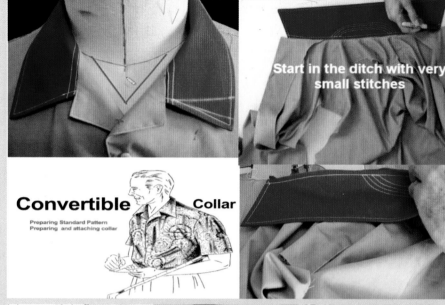

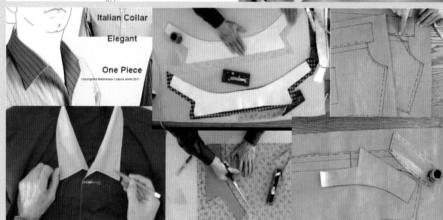

Men's Shirt Catalogue | Men's sport shirts, Japanese style. Much as I liked the Shimazaki Ryuichiro book I mentioned in the dress-shirt Resources, I like this one even better; it has more varied garments and better how-to images.

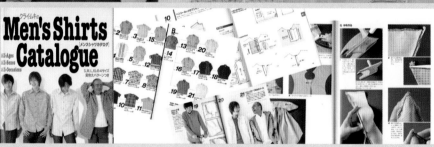

My Favorite Shirt, by Machiko Kayaki. This is pretty much the women's sport shirt version of the previous book and the colors reflect the style differences; lovely simple garments here, lots of detail and block variety (but only the garment titles are translated!).

To Consider

Gaze a moment at the diagrams below, saying softly to yourself, "These are all exactly the same." Close your eyes and recall that every collar in this entire chapter is either a combination or a camp, and then imagine that the jacket chapter is full of shawls (it is). Finally, open up your eyes again and look at the last figure, in pink, saying, "That's a facing-collar combo that could become an inset front panel." Before long, you'll hear a soft bell tinkling.

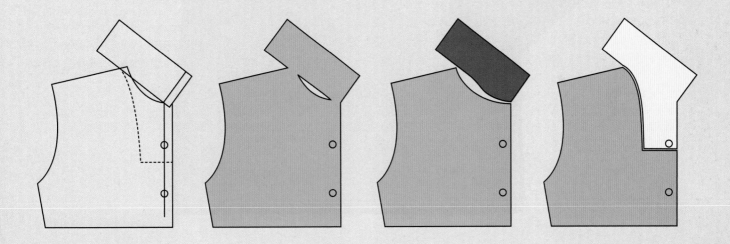

The 1950s-era body shirt at left is here simply to make a point. It's a clammy pure petroleum knit with a combo collar straight out of the sport-shirt chapter and sleeve plackets and cuffs right out of the dress-shirt chapter, packed with indestructible synthetic canvas interfacings that simulate a good starching.

Much more intriguing to me are the two garments below, fully explored online. Christine Jonson's shirt is from her pattern, Straight Shirt 723, which is a basic sport shirt with convertible collar and the body scaled and shaped for a beefy, lycra-blended ponte. In

every respect it is made like its woven counterpart, with front and back facings, but has a plain hemmed sleeve finish. Simple and sumptuous. Christine's collar/CF construction process is recapped online, with additional examples.

Then there's this J. Peterman rugby shirt with woven collar and placket (twill tape reinforced), a woven shoulder lining layer that's quilted to the soft jersey body, and dyed-to-match ribbed cuffs. A similar collar and neckline construction process is detailed online.

Garments Profiled Online:

Christine Jonson Straight Shirt

J Peterman Padded Shoulder Sweatshirt

All the styles and details shown here are profiled online with complete directions for construction.

A classic ready-to-wear type-4 polo placket and bound neckline suitable for both purchased and assembled knit collars.

Two options for combining woven and partially woven collars and plackets on knit bodies, based on these lovely washable-wool polo shirts from Australian Jill Atherton's Infinity Cottage Studio workshop.

A pure twill tape placket with a rectangular folded-over knit collar from the body fabric.

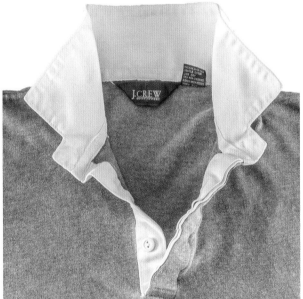

An ultra-classic woven rugby collar with a cut-on stand, and a type-2 continuous-band woven placket with an inserted button strip.

Observe the pure rectangles that form this shirt's body, armholes, sleeve caps, and even the triangular underarm inserts. See the folk-shirt chapter for details.

Barbour Polar Quilt Jacket

At left is my favorite knit/woven combo shirt-jacket, from fleece and waxed-cotton fabrics quilted together all over and bound with twill tape. At the plain rectangular collar and snap-on throat latch, corduroy is layered over the quilting and similarly bound with tape. The patch pockets and the zipper-covering flap are made from the same fleece/cotton combination.

Below, fleece designer and author Rochelle Harper works an exactly similar concept at home with fleece free-hand quilted to

Supplex, the edges bound with a micro-fleece strip. She explains, "To eliminate any shifting during the quilting, lightly bond the layers with Misty Fuse, an ultra-fine fusible web that adds very little stiffness and no bulk to the layers. To protect the heat-sensitive fleece, pre-fuse the web to the non-fleece layer using a Teflon sheet, then lightly and carefully tack that to the fleece layer, with another fleece layer underneath all, to protect the fleece nap. Be careful not to stretch the knit while bonding, and stitch with the woven on top. Staystitch the edges before binding."

Despite fleece's stretch and softness, Rochelle generally prefers not to serge any but the lightest varieties, because the bulk makes serged seams almost as prominent and stiff as piping. At left she's used a double-stitched welt seam with plain straight stitches from a regular machine. A loose honeycomb stretch stitch, also shown at left, works perfectly when attaching the patch pockets. At the top of the seam, which is the pocket mouth on the front, she's switched to a loose satin stitch that acts like a big bar tack to reinforce the opening.

More woven layering and quilting over fleece, these are turned facings small enough to require no bonding first.

To create an elastic edging, doubled-over swimsuit Lycra is commonly used to bind fleece edges. The twin raw edges are stitched down first on the wrong side, then the folded edge is caught with in-the-ditch stitching, also stitched from the wrong side, all while stretching the Lycra.

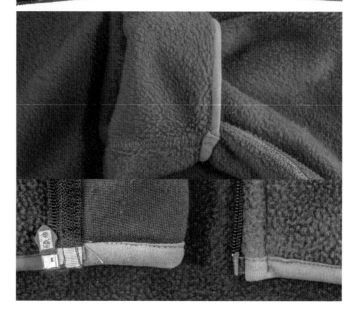

Profiled Online

Outerwear designer at Woolrich until recently, Valerie Beggs also prefers not to serge fleece seams. Instead, she developed the method shown on this shirt from her Woodland Waders line: the fleece edges are lapped very slightly at each seam line, after satin-edging the lower layer with a serger. To join them, she simply zigzagged over the layered edges; after an initial shedding when cut, fleece doesn't ravel. For the corduroy bindings, she again pre-serged to edge the inner edge, straight-stitched the plain edge right sides together to the garment front, wrapped, then secured through all layers with a simple, light zigzag.

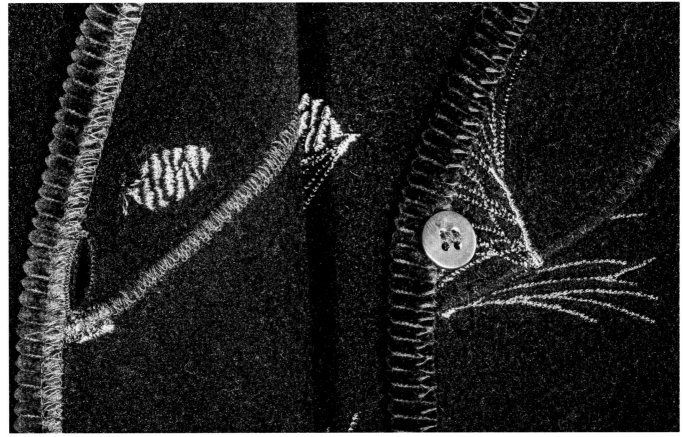

Sew the New Fleece, by Rochelle Harper. There's no better reference guide to fleece garment techniques.

Singer Sewing with Knits | Among the vast array of generally fine knit-sewing guides, this beautifully photographed Singer volume stands out for its extensive coverage of no-serger workarounds. As Rochelle told me, "The only reason to insist on serged seams for knit sewing is when you demand high stretch and full recovery." On less stressed knit garments, straight stitches can work fine. Marcy Tilton, among many other knit experts, only uses sergers as edge-finishing tools.

Cjpatterns.com | Christine Jonson's popular patterns are specially crafted for her favorite fabrics, Lycra-blended knits. Best of all, she carries a reliably consistent collection of these fabrics by the yard, so you can often come back and get more of something you fall in love with.

Fusible fabric spray | Marcy Tilton keeps odorless, colorless, acid-free, temporary, and repositionable 505 fabric spray adhesive handy for tacking knit hems before stitching them with a double needle. She sprays right at her cutting table, as shown in the center image at right, with the work in a small box to catch any overspray, which is generally minimal.

Both 505 and Misty Fuse are widely available, as well as direct from the makers' websites.

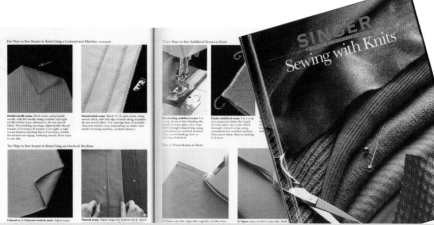

To Consider

Garments Profiled Online

Check out these high-action performance tops that mix knits with wovens for maximum movement with trim fit. At right is a woven equestrian competition shirt designed to be worn under a formal riding jacket, concealing the Lycra-knit side and underarm panels.

At right is a military-approved combat uniform shirt with a knit body and under-arm panels, heavy woven upper sleeve layers sporting multiple zippered pockets and shoulder- and elbow-padding insert panels, and a woven rectangular band collar and zipper placket. Note also the deep ribbed cuffs with thumbholes left in the seams. The whole thing is designed to be worn under body armor, and the woven material is so stiff as to feel like armor itself, but the concept is fascinating, even for less demanding activities.

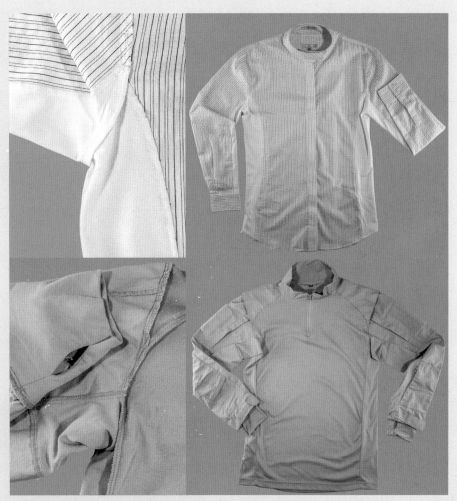

CHAPTER 6

The Folk
(or Rectangular)
Shirt Block

Another short chapter, this one's here because this ancient and venerable shape is so . . . ancient and venerable. And potentially great looking, as well as amazingly comfortable. It's also connected to garments with a lot of interesting details and treatments that are pure history, pure shirt, and purely fun to explore on any block.

The block fits if you can get it on and aren't swimming inside it. My opinion is that these shapes look and feel best when rather snug in the chest and close at the underarms. But consider the kimono, or any of the other Japanese variants (karate coats, etc.), which fit only when wrapped with a belt. The list goes on.

The signature details and features here include the completely unshaped, uncurved seams, everywhere except sometimes there's a simple curved neckline; even the folded-square gussets at the underarm and sometimes side vents. Any kind of collar or opening at the neck could be used. Shoulders, being completely square, are often unseamed, the body being just a folded-over rectangle. Often there's an extra yoke-like layer reinforcing and adding insulation to the shoulders and upper chest. Historical examples are often joined with butted seams, the edges being selvedges rather than cut, and thus safely and quite elegantly whipped together without even an overlap, for the least bulky seams possible. But the core detail is sleeves thrusting outward from the body at exactly or nearly a right angle. Any garment with sleeves that do this is recalling this heritage, even if the shoulders aren't perfectly square, and whether anybody notices or not. Maybe now you will.

Another element I find appealing here is the persistent whisper that you could probably make something very like this, and very wearable, without any pattern at all, just a circumference and a length measure, and a needle. And that somebody a thousand years ago no doubt did just that with a knotted string to take the measurements.

More practically, I like the idea of swiping details from these boxcar togs for use on more contemporary blocks, or adding more sophisticated collars, hoods, and closures to the original. And for the reminder that squared-off sleeve caps and armholes aren't at all a bad idea, certainly not on working clothes.

My next-door neighbor owns this shirt, apparently the national garment in New Zealand, where he got it. He claims he's never once worn it in public without somebody stopping him to find out where to get one (they're still being made and sold worldwide). I believe him; it's just what I did, except I also insisted he take it off and let me photograph it inside and out.

No secrets here, just plain sewing and obvious structures. The front isn't even a placket, just a faced slit with a faced flap behind. The hood is the only part that you might pause over before completely understanding. Actually, I guess there is a secret, but it's in the "100-year-old secret method" for waterproofing of the all-wool fabric, not the construction.

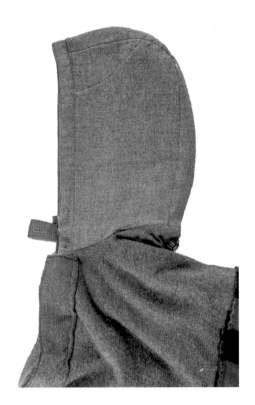

Meanwhile, back in the Old Country, folk of all persuasions are still wearing and loving this all-rectangles fisherman's smock, born and first worn in Cornwall, UK. It's even simpler than the bush shirt, with no gussets except at the boat-neck collar, a slight acknowledgment that shoulders slope. No shoulder seams, though. And no edge finishing inside, although on one side, the fabric selvedge is at the garment edge. Note how the underarm allowances are clipped right to the seam, in lieu of those gussets I suppose, and with apparently perfect confidence that everything will be well anyway, so go ahead and fish. It certainly feels good on.

The collar options (again all from rectangular parts) from the maker of my smock are recapped in the drawings below, and they look familiar, no? The last one on the right is meant to represent the zippered coat version, pulling these things on over your head being the main awkwardness they present. But once on, the absence of any opening feels very comforting. Schematics and even drafts for garments like these are easy to find online, and I've captured a few links for you in my online stash.

Here's an obvious U.S. heir to the folk shirt, updated with a simple cut to the shoulders, an arm drop, and a little curve to the sleeves and armholes. Built from army blankets, it has some slightly fancy hardware at the hem and cuffs, and the throat lacing tightens by pulling down instead of up, a blindingly obvious notion. It's hard to show, but the kangaroo pocket is not as simple as it appears, having been divided up inside with multiple patch pockets, including one exactly iPhone size on the outer layer, and a large zippered one on the body side. There's also two tabs in there with nylon D-rings for clipping important stuff to; somebody rightly likened this to feeling like you're wearing an office desk as you trek the wild, but that pales compared to the sense of walking around inside a body-sized house; this thing is warm! Note how Empire's much more sophisticated offering, the Grey Fox pullover shown below and profiled online retains the folk arm and shoulder shape despite being cut up into lots of mysterious seams, none of which are unfinished.

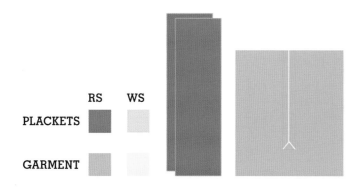

	RS	WS
PLACKETS		
GARMENT		

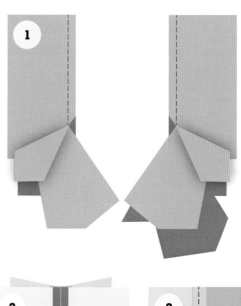

Centered Outside Faced Slash

Inspired by a favorite garment like the Folkwear pattern below, I played around with the type-1 placket structure and came up with a slightly different way of creating Folkwear's View A closure, as well as a simple way to replicate any variation on the other views, either centered or offset to one side, at right.

1 With all pieces right sides up, join each placket piece to one edge of the slash, which should be about 1 inch (2.5 cm) wide, stopping and backstitching at the clipping.

2 On the wrong side, arrange each placket so it folds in the center of the opening, exactly meeting the other one. Press to make creases at the folds.

3 Fold the placket layers right sides together with the edges aligned, then stitch along the crease mark from the bottom up to just slightly beyond the earlier stitching and backstitch.

4 Press the garment and placket layers open and finish, then secure the edges.

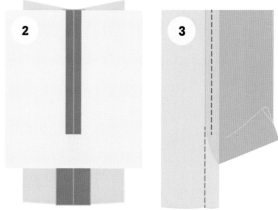

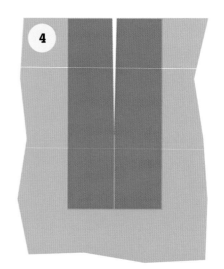

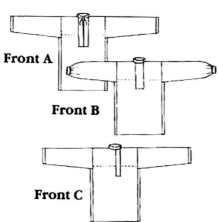

Front A

Front B

Front C

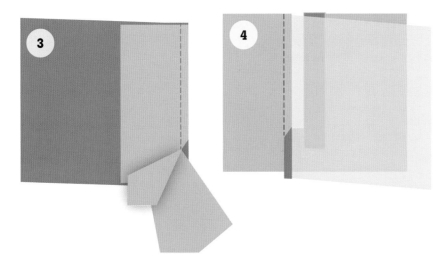

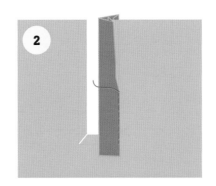

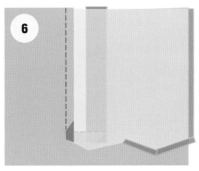

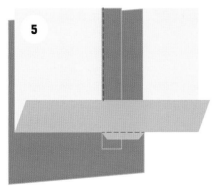

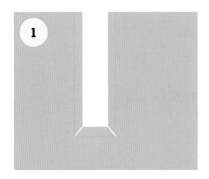

Design-It-as-You-Go Placket Opening

This is a good process to try in muslin. You can eyeball the width and shape of the overlap as you form it, then position the whole thing as you like over your block neckline to transfer that back to your placket layers.

1 Mark and slash an opening as shown, 2 to 3 inches (5.1 to 7.6 cm) wide.

2 Cut and join a narrowish placket rectangle as shown, stitching to the clipping.

3 Cut another placket piece at least three times as wide as the slash and a few inches longer. Join as shown, both right sides up, stopping at the clip.

4 Fold the large placket on its seam entirely to the right side. If necessary, arrange the small placket's lower end so it's also entirely on the right side below the stitches.

5 On the wrong side, flip the garment up so the unstitched edge of the slash can fold down over the placket layers. Stitch through all layers as shown, then fold the garment back down flat.

6 Now from the right side you can start playing with the ways the large placket piece might best fold over the layers below it. Note that it doesn't need to start to fold back at the under-placket's edge or finish up at the slash on the other side. Nor does it have to fold in straight edges. It might curve as suggested in figure 7. You should also have a better idea now of how you might want to cut another set of test pieces to get closer to what you want. Note that you could also cut a shape into the overlap's outer edge and seam a new upper piece onto it instead of simply folding it back on itself, as described on page 42 for type-3 placket variations.

Kayla Kennington

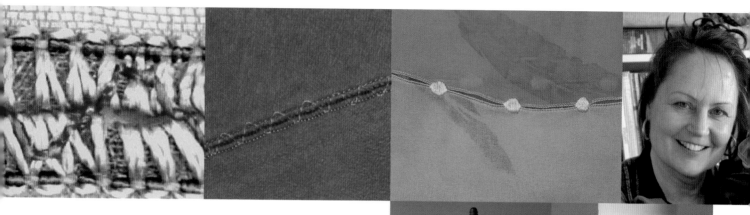

Textile artist, dye master, machine embroidery wizard, and pattern designer Kayla Kennington has been pushing the rectangle as a garment core for her whole extraordinary career. (She's the only designer ever to be honorably disqualified from further entries in the international Bernina Design Competition, for having won Grand Prize in both of the first two years the competition ran; after that all her entries were juried in as "honorary.") All of her Modular Design sewing patterns (sewingpatterns.com) and most of her client and personal creations are built up from mostly rectangular "modules" with completely finished edges that butt together to be joined in a multitude of ways, as shown in the seam-line close-ups above. I love how the swirly hem of the gauzy black silk "shirt" at bottom left simply grew from the same triangle-gusseted rectangles we saw at the sides of the Swanndri bush shirt, scaled up and divided about three times. Simple and timeless magic indeed!

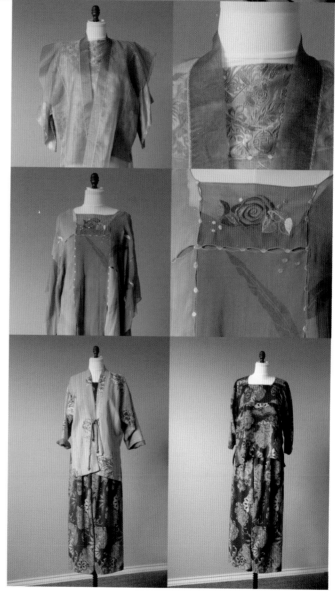

Folk (or Rectangular) Block

These two books showcase the rectangular garment's history in very distinct, equally fascinating, ways.

Patterns of Fashion, by Janet Arnold. Janet's approach is born from her extensive and exquisite documentation of Elizabethan courtly costume, complete with patterns and enough detail to allow very precise recreations. Packed with gorgeous drawings and photos, this is one of my most inspiring and treasured costume books. It's volume 4 in her monumental and celebrated series, and it's largely devoted to shirts and robes, all rectangular.

Cut My Cote, by Dorothy Burnham. This book takes the folk approach, following the rectangular garment around the globe, with less lavish but equally useful diagrams, good enough to be used as patterns, or simply inspiration and enlightenment concerning our rectangular roots.

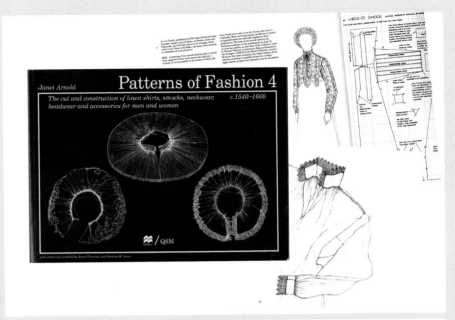

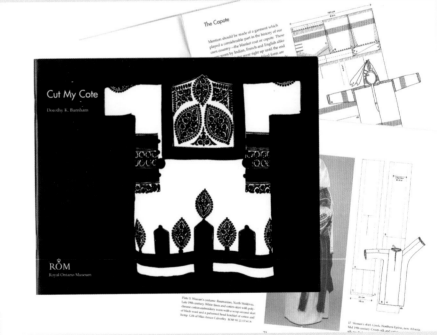

Pattern-Free Fashion, by Mary Lee Trees Cole. Want to try a square shirt? This how-to book, or pretty much any Folkwear pattern from their Old Europe or Asian collections, would be a great starting point. I really like these Old German smocks along with the Russian shirts I presented a few pages back. And the bodies are a nicely sophisticated variants on plain rectangles.

148 — BLACK FOREST SMOCK

This traditional smock was called a *Kittel*, or over-garment, worn by workers in Germany, Switzerland, and France. Soft pleats fall from a wide neckband. Sleeves connect to side panels with gussets and are pleated at the wrists into buttoned cuff bands. Shoulder yokes, pocket welts, neckband, and cuffs were often decorated with chain-stitching (design and instructions are included inside pattern).

Our Black Forest Smock can be worn by men as an over-shirt, and by women as a mid-calf length dress. Make it for the kids with **#110 Little Kittel.**

Front & Back Views

Shirt Length

Front

Dress Length

Back

SUGGESTED FABRICS

Soft or crisp fabrics such as linen, homespun, broadcloth, gingham, denim, featherweight corduroy, or lightweight wool.

MATERIALS FOR OPTIONAL EMBROIDERY

See **Instructions for Embroidery** inside pattern cover.

BLACK FOREST SMOCK

To Consider

The mission here is simply to allow oneself to notice ever more examples of, or at least hints of, the folk rectangle in modern clothing and patterns. Things that work tend to persist!

CHAPTER 7

The Shirt-Jacket (or Oversized) Block

The Shirt-Jacket

Garments of this type include all kinds of coats and jackets for both indoor and outdoor use.

What I'm calling a shirt-jacket commonly has these features:

Fit

These bodies are sized to fit easily over other garments or layers. My preference as a block source would as usual be to copy a comfortable overshirt or jacket body. Some old tailor's drafts I've seen recommend that overcoats be built on measurements two sizes up from the body measures used for suit jackets. With the same logic, one might start a shirt-jacket block from a shirt pattern one or two sizes up from what you'd choose for a dress shirt. Equally, any traditional jacket or coat pattern or draft could be treated as a block source and adapted to a shirt-like treatment. In my vision, this means anything simpler than full-on tailoring; no stretching or shrinking to shape the fabric; with no body interfacings or fixed roll lines; and with linings, if any, that simply repeat and underlie the body shapes, and are likely to be partial or just extended facings. Necklines are usually bigger all around the neck compared to those on next-to-the-body blocks, and may drop further down the chest or be raised toward the chin as desired to suit any collar shape or fabric weight. The degree of weather protection wanted—from none to serious—will probably be the main factor driving size and ease, with more being needed for heavier layers, of course.

Details

As you'll see from the example at left and its details on the next spreads, any loose enough sport shirt with a convertible collar could be directly translated into one sort of shirt-jacket with almost no pattern changes. But any kind of collar or none can work. Here, I'll focus on the common shaping and scaling effects commonly applied to collar types we've seen in other block chapters to adapt them to outerwear. Yokes are not typical but not out of place, and are sometimes scaled up and extended to serve as additional weather barriers for the upper back and shoulders. Summer-y layers with short or shortened sleeves are feasible, too. Long or short, sleeves may be split or shaped into upper and under pieces, with any sort of cuff or sleeve hem finish. Hems are usually unshaped and not expected to be tucked in.

Pockets, both inside and out, are expected and common at waist and chest level, and scaled up as suits outerwear. Hoods, attached or removable, are certainly common, but not featured here, as patterns are already widely available.

Fabrics

Fabrics can be woven or knit, or multilayered or mixed, and are more likely than not to be medium- or heavy-weight, crisp or soft. Washability is not crucial. Water and wind resistance may be wanted.

I consider this classic a case study in the transformation of a simple convertible-collar shirt into a soft sort of unstructured sport coat. I've tried to capture here every detail that went into the rethink. Start with the extended self-fabric facing that joins the lining fabric yoke at the shoulder, neither of which are attached at any point to the front or back body pieces except at the neck and armholes (you can run your arm completely from front to back underneath them). Move on to the classic shirt sleeves joined just like on a dress shirt with flat-felled seams at the armholes, catching the facing and yoke layers.

Move down the uninterfaced facing to the hem, pausing to take in the simple machine-rolled edge that finishes it at right, then continue on to the transition from facing to hem fold that circles around to the unvented side seams and across the single back piece. Continue down the sleeves to the totally traditional, quite soft shirt cuffs crossing over the pleated sleeve ends, and then flip the continuous strip type-2 plackets over a few times, noting how they've been edgestitched to hold them in a less freewheeling—not to say less feminine—more dressed for dinner at the cabin manner. Roll a big leather button between your fingers once or twice thinking about long-ago fashions for such things, and then it's back up to the collar for the Big Question: Is even that interfaced? I can't bear to pick a seam, but it feels exactly like the unfettered "lapel" right next to it, and there's nothing poking out between the allowances under the yoke. But really, does it matter? You and I will each do whatever we want when we adapt this idea to our own ends, yes? Thank you, nameless Pendleton designer who created this answer to one of my personal life questions within a year of my own creation. Of course, I'll probably choose a different collar shape, and maybe less shirt-y cuffs.

Straight

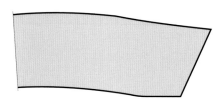

Curved

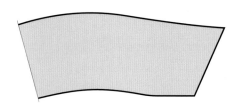

Partial Stand

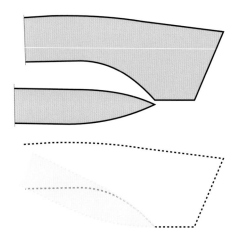

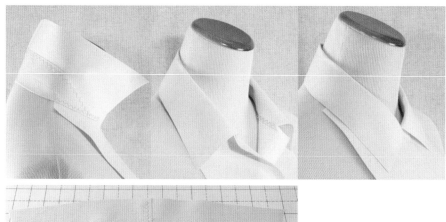

As we've already seen with sport-block convertible collars, nothing much needs be done to make these go sort of lapel-like. But jacket designers have long preferred to do some things to make the distinction more certain. First, they tend to up the scale if nothing else, as in the example at left labeled **Straight**, which is otherwise shaped very much like sport convertible patterns 6, 7, and 8 from pages 90-91, just bigger all around.

More dramatically, they'll introduce a slight downward curve around the shoulder to cause the collar to lie more platelike and less cylindrically around the neck, as in the **Curved** example, all the better to show off the back of a cylinder collar that might be worn beneath it.

Introducing a **Partial Stand** allows for some curve difference to appear at the roll-line fold, as the curves between the stand and the collar are different. And see how the collar does seem to both stand up in back and lie flat in front at the same time? It's subtle, but it's there.

At right, you'll note this **Cut-On Stand** collar's more deeply dipping-down neckline edge, as well as the flattened neckline on the jacket. This reshaping redirects the seam line between them to cut more across the lapel than parallel to it, an altogether more jacket-like effect. Note that for this example I've also added a down-curved variation, like the curved shape at far left, which drops the whole thing back down onto the shoulders and off the neck as before, requiring that the whole collar outer edge be trimmed to return the collar depth to something more proportionate.

Cut-On Stand

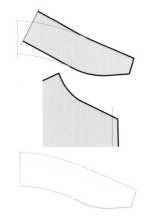

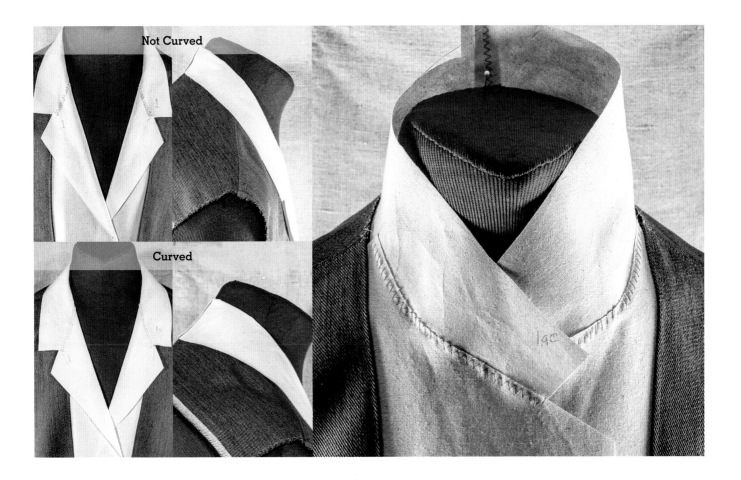

Not Curved

Curved

Conv A

Conv B

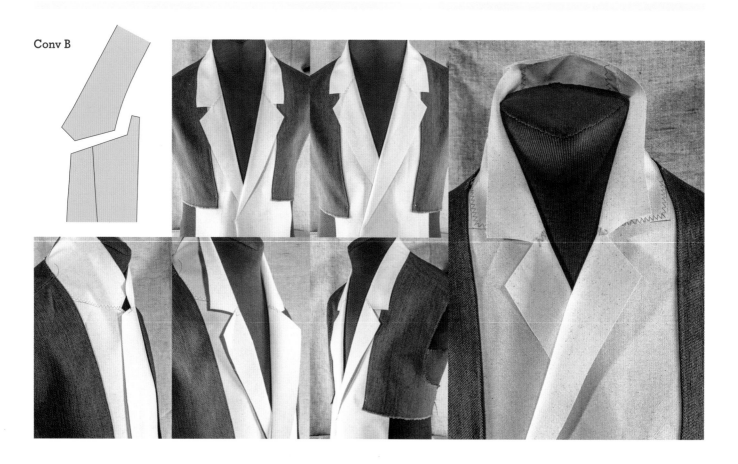

Here are further examples of more dramatic convertible-collar rescalings and reshapings for more jacket-like results.

Double Breasted

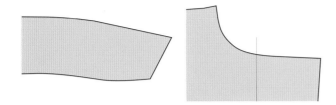

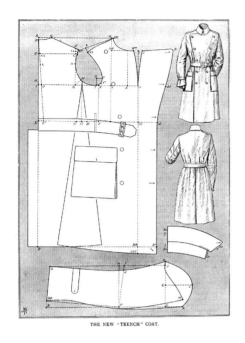

THE NEW "TRENCH" COAT.

Collars with dress-shirt-like stands and falls can be equally reshaped and scaled for outerwear. The effect is commonly seen on trench coats, examples at left, all on the same neckline, as illustrated at example Tr1 below. Usually these trench stands end at center-front without an overlap, sometimes with wire hooks and eyes to secure them, and often with throat latches to button or buckle across the neck.

At right is a completely different take, also built on a shaped stand, inspired by designer Nigel Cabourn's recent Debenham collar, itself inspired by an early twentieth-century seaman's jacket. See more examples on my Pinterest jacket board.

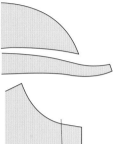

Deb 1

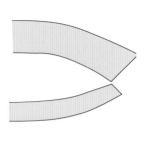

Tr 1

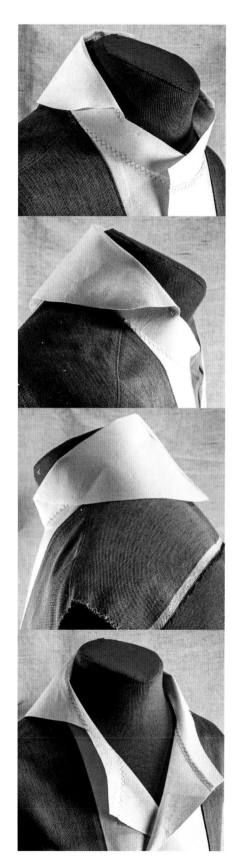

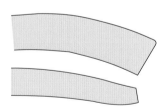

Tr 2

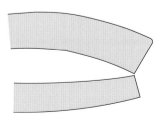

Tr 3

Here's a quite different reworking of a convertible-collar shirt into serious outerwear, although the first thing you notice isn't likely to be the quite ordinary shirt-like collar; it's that cape-like double layering across the shoulders, chest, and back, right? (This reminds me a bit of the Swanndri bush shirt's double-layered shoulders.) Note how this one-piece plaid layer goes bias after crossing the sloped shoulders onto the front and then wraps under the sleeves.

The double layering continues below the cape with the layered pockets, front and back. In back there's a huge game or map pocket extending across the full width of the back and almost the full length from hem to cape. Underneath the cape, the maker ditches the pretty blue fabric for an equally heavy plain black wool for the hidden sleeve layer. Inside lower left you can also see that the collar and facing are exactly the same as on any other convertible-collared shirt. The collar geek in me finds the best bit to be how the under-collar's neckline edge, at lower right, has been serged to finish it so it can simply overlap the neckline rather than being tucked inside this already way-bulky seam line.

Despite how shirt-like this noble creation appears to me in my shirt-fixated state, Filson recognizes it as a "mackinaw." They certainly ought to know! I suppose that's a sort of short coat body style, as we'll see next. As usual, I'm all about the collars and will let the body (just a big rectangle here as most everywhere else in this book) slide.

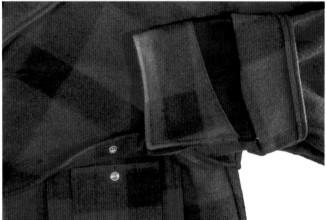

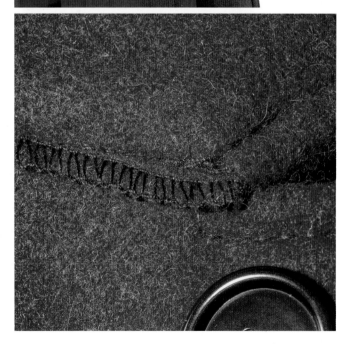

Mackinaw Collars

In an old Harry Simons book on coat drafts I found the image below, as well as a draft that caught my eye as a nice shawl collar shape. In my digital way, I scanned, traced, and scaled this up to more or less my own size, and cut some muslins. The first, Sim 1, below, was rather modestly scaled but still with width enough for a double-breasted treatment. I enjoyed the scale but felt it needed to be bigger for the full mackinaw effect, so I dragged the outline bigger in Illustrator; Sim 2 is at right. Note that I also decided to convert this outline to a partial stand, just to see what that did.

For one thing, it created a seam line across the shawl curve, which you can see shifting as I try out different center-front opening depths. Scale is better!

Referring back to the Simons diagram, I note that the shawl and notched collars there are much the same. So let's have some notches in my shawl, each a little different. Note that I chose to follow the seam line, which was somewhat arbitrary; these notches could have been placed anywhere or angled differently, but as cut, they maintain the original neckline curve, which works out rather well when crossing the center-fronts up close to the neck. Also note that to get the flat-on-the-shoulders effect depicted in the finished garment drawings, the back necks of these collar drafts should be curved down, as described on page 155. These straight-back collar shapes will always stand up close to the neck.

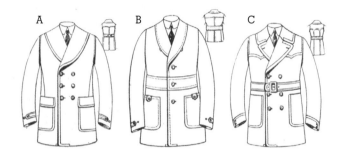

A. Double-breasted shawl collar mackinaw
B. Single-breasted shawl collar mackinaw
C. Double-breasted convertible collar mackinaw

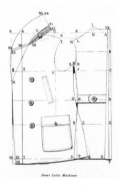

Shawl Collar Mackinaw

Sim 1

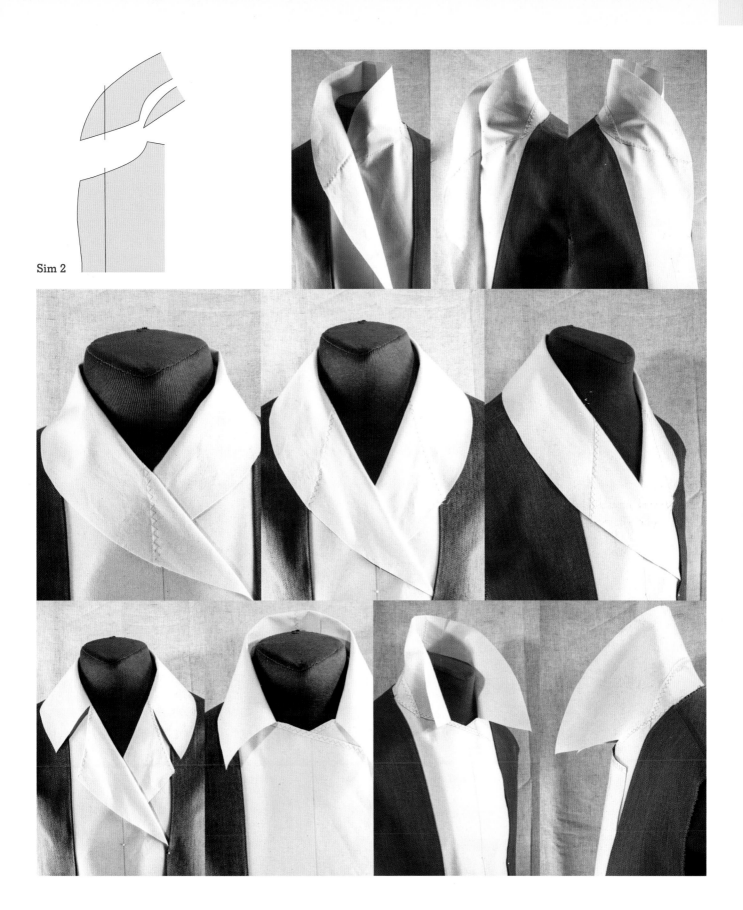

Sim 2

Featured Patterns   Shawl Collars 🖨

Shawl collars scale up and down quite well, going from slim blouse effects to the serious business of the Simons one just chopped up. Here, let's go down in scale and play with height and edge shapes.

Below, Sh1 has a deep neck and a sharp downward angle, still allowing for a pleasing, high-buttoned effect, I think, but best at dropping lower.

For Sh2 I chopped into the curve, lowering the back neck height without lowering in front.

Sh3 takes a further notch away.

Sh 1

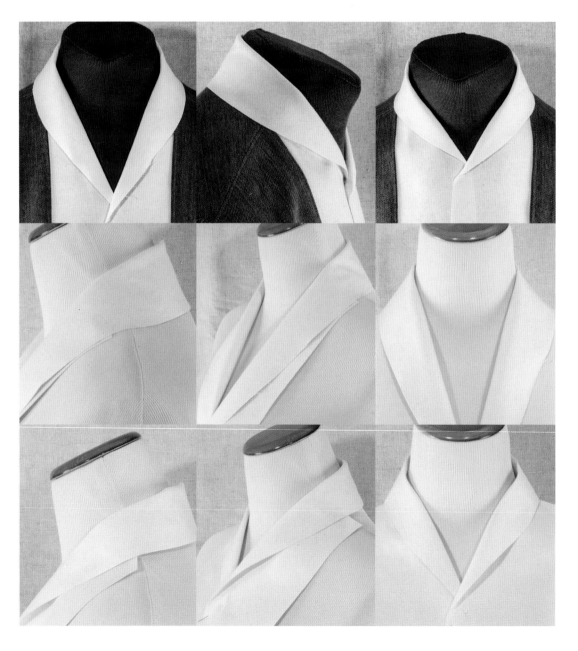

Sh 2

Sh 3

Sh 4

Sh4 is a new lower draft slightly angled up compared to Sh1.

And Sh5 goes back to a deep neck, but with a raised angle, going for a better high-neck result, which I think I got.

Sh 5

Online Featured Garments

Orvis Canvas Travel Jacket

Before I got my 49er jacket, this was the garment I intended as a prototype for my own "sport-coat shirt." The Pendelton is an even easier route, but this one is full of interesting ideas, too, plus lots of pockets.

Author-Made Folkwear Australian Drovers Coat

I added quite a few tweaks to this wonderfully simple and functional design, fully detailed with new pattern pieces online.

L.L. Bean Canvas Barn Coat with Button-in Lining

I thought it would be the pockets I found most interesting about this classic design, but it turned out to be the unique bi-swing back shapes and the simple method for integrating a removable lining.

Author-Made Tweed Jacket with Knit Sleeves

Not an unqualified success, but pretty close! Join me as I see whether I can fix this oddball thing. Fully lined and underlined, with cashmere machine-knit sleeves, it's worth saving.

Landau Lab Coat 29083

When the doc entered the room, I knew right away what I really needed: a good look inside his lab coat.

Finally, let's return to the idea of layering, in contrast to lining, as a way of adding function to shirts intended as outerwear. The Drover's coat from Folkwear has a classic straight, short rain cape that snaps on or off and is held down with simple straps under the arms. I layered mine with a high-tech rainproof synthetic, and it certainly keeps the rain out. Note that I also cut the sleeves so they wouldn't join at the armpits for more ventilation.

Below that is an interesting if not entirely successful reversible shirt from Territory Ahead. It does certainly reverse, and it's pretty clear how they handled all the edges to allow that (the bigger images online show these off well). I admire the double-faced continuous strips and perfectly aligned pocket patches! The problem, no doubt fixable, is with the buttons, which are just linked pairs with a 3/8-inch (1-cm) thread chain between. These should work, but they prove annoyingly awkward in practice, and are not aided by the too-tight buttonholes; details!

At right, my cavalry-twill panel shirt has a few bulk-reduction and convenience features that come from inner layers. Obviously, a thinner cotton inner layer at the collar and front panels lightens things up well, but so do the faced hems, cuffs, and plackets. It's more pleasant to wear, and easier to sew as well. The silk-lined sleeves facilitate slipping this tunic on and off, but they were a bear to sew. I tried to simply treat the two layers as one, which mostly worked, but it began to fail at the flat-felled armhole seams. Next time I'll do a lined sleeve's caps in two passes instead one. There's always something to do better next time!

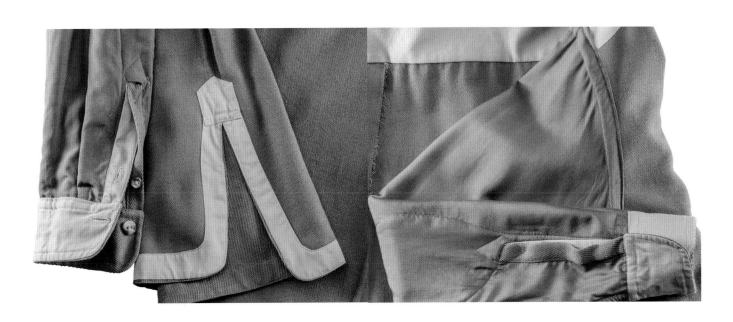

Men's Coat Book, by Ryuichiro Shimazaki. This book is filled with perfect reproductions of many classic designs, and like all the other Japanese titles here, comes complete with full-size patterns and quite clear, if tiny, construction diagrams.

The Japanese Pattern Challenge is home to a blogging seamster who's worked his way through every garment in it.

Thread Theory, the pattern line from the Merediths, featured in the Skills chapter, brought in a tailoring expert as a guest blogger for a thorough sew-along on working up their Goldstream Peacoat pattern as a hand-tailoring project.

Sew Better, Sew Faster: Garment Industry Secrets | Margaret Islander's niece Janet Prey continues her legacy as a convincing, and captivating, proponent of industrial sewing techniques. In her Craftsy class she uncovers worker-wear construction with this heavily topstitched and rugged jeans-type shirt-jacket.

The Japanese Pattern Challenge

To Consider

If, like me, you're a little more interested in unique and streamlined projects than in classic tailoring, at least when it comes to shirt-jackets, I can definitely recommend these *Threads* articles on one-layer sewing.

Issue #103: "Lapped Seam Construction" by Kathryn Brenne brings raw-edged, unlined, fast but precise outerwear construction into plausible focus, perfect for ravel-free fabrics like double cloth, melton, and felted wool jersey, plus even some fleeces. I'm game, and Kathryn's a wiz.

Issue #104: And here she is again, demystifying shearling, yet another prospect for the techniques above, or not. Under her tutelage I made a shearling coat and love it. NOT that hard.

Issue #109: If those sound interesting, don't miss Karen Tornow on felting wool jersey. In my book, she OWNS this technique!

About the Author

David Page Coffin is an artist, writer, photographer, illustrator, and garment maker living on the Oregon coast with his artist wife, Ellen, who took the photo shown here. The idea to start sewing clothes didn't come to him until his mid-20s, and it continues to surprise him that deciding to do that led to all the best jobs he's ever been involved in, before or since, including producing this book with the great team at Creative Publishing international. He was an editor at Threads magazine for eighteen years, which led to his meeting and learning from all the contributors mentioned and unmentioned in these pages. The author of two previous sewing books (Shirtmaking, Taunton Press 1992; and Making Trousers for Men and Women, CPi 2009), and many articles for Threads, David has taught and lectured all over the U.S., Canada, and the U.K. He has also taught an online class for Craftsy.com, been a frequent guest host on several online sewing forums, and has hosted live chats on PatternReview.com. He has appeared on Sandra Betzina's HGTV sewing program, and his instructional videos have been broadcast on YouTube.com, generating great reviews on ThreadBanger.com, PatternReview.com, and other sewing sites. David hosts the following online sites:

www.shirtmakingwithdpc.com

http://makingtrouserswithdpc.blogspot.com

http://myvirtualworkshop.blogspot.com

Index